soul
growth
astrology

soul growth astrology

A Workbook for Realizing Your Soul's True Desires

MOLLY McCORD

Author of *Awakening Astrology*

Hierophantpublishing

Cover design by Laura Beers
Cover art by Lera Efremova | Shutterstock
Page vi astrology chart by Lina Keil c/o Shutterstock.com
Chapter head images by Creative Illustrator c/o Shutterstock.com
Print book interior design by Frame25 Productions

Hierophant Publishing
San Antonio, TX
www.hierophantpublishing.com

If you are unable to order this book from your
local bookseller, you may order directly from the publisher.

ISBN: 978-1-950253-47-0

10 9 8 7 6 5 4 3 2 1

This book is dedicated to every soul courageously moving into the glory of their astrological energies during one of the most pivotal times on this planet. You've totally got this.

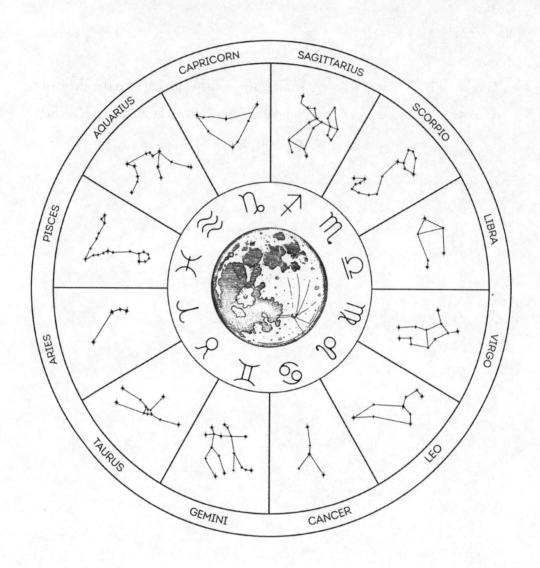

Contents

Foreword

My love for astrology began over forty years ago. As a rebellious, punk-rock-loving teenager, I was interested in all things that were considered taboo at the time, and when a friend's mother (a fifty-something astrologer herself) gave me a reading, my mind was blown at the depth and accuracy of the information she provided. I felt truly *seen* for the first time. This reading sparked a life-long interest in the subject that has led to a flourishing career as an astrologer, author, and teacher.

Consequently, some of you reading this may assume that I've exhausted all there is to know on the topic by now, or that I know myself so well there is no need to seek. I can close the books and charts and be satisfied with what I already know about astrology . . . and myself.

Wrong!

Astrology and self-discovery are never-ending journeys, and one thing I've learned is that there is always something new to discover. Thankfully, astrologers like Molly McCord are showing seekers new ways to use astrology for personal growth and transformation.

Like me, Molly was drawn to astrology at an early age. Before long, her passion became a vocation—and her life's mission. She has helped thousands of people learn to live their best lives through her astrological consultations. Her first book, *Awakening Astrology*, and the workbook in your hands are both filled with astrological wisdom we can all apply to our lives.

In *Soul Growth Astrology*, Molly moves beyond basic astrological information and takes you on a deep dive into the twelve Zodiac signs. Instead of teaching only the basics about each sign, she offers lessons, exercises, journal prompts, and wise guidance to help you understand, love, and heal yourself.

While you may assume this is strictly a Sun-sign book, it isn't. Molly advises you to read about the signs that rule every aspect of your natal chart. For example, although I'm a Gemini Sun, my Moon is in Scorpio, and I have a cluster of planets in Virgo. As I read through each section, I once again felt seen, much as I had in my first reading so long ago.

The book begins with a story about caterpillars growing inside their cocoons. At some point, the encasement becomes too small. The caterpillar struggles as it breaks through the barriers of the cocoon, finally emerging as a butterfly. As it spreads its wings, it's ready to fly.

Molly compares this process to the soul's journey. Astrology can help bring about great transformation once you understand what your soul is here to do. This book provides the wisdom you need to reach your soul's full potential.

In many ways, I'm still very much that rebellious punk-rock teenager who discovered astrology all those years ago, but now I'm back in the cocoon as I prepare for my next journey as a senior citizen. Although I sometimes feel scared about that prospect, the knowledge I've gained in *Soul Growth Astrology* will help me transcend those fears and face my upcoming metamorphosis with courage and clarity. May it guide you through yours as well.

—Theresa Reed, author of *Astrology for Real Life*

Introduction

The Soul Growth Journey

A restlessness stirs in the caterpillar's heart. The tightly woven cocoon she once experienced as a nurturing womb has now become tight and confining. Almost in spite of herself, she begins to move and push, stretching against the boundaries of her silky encasement. She can feel deep in her cells that it is time to change. She can feel, with every beat of her heart, that it is time to grow. Without quite knowing why, she gives a little shake. Suddenly, she becomes aware of the furled wings bundled up at her sides, wet and raw as fresh paint. She gives another shake, and the misty white chrysalis surrounding her begins to tear apart.

It feels messy, sticky, uncomfortable, and strange. But within a few minutes, she emerges as a beautiful butterfly, her wings unfurled in a mosaic, her antennae reaching out to greet the world. After a long period of solitude during which she felt her entire identity dissolve—and in which she had no choice but to surrender completely to mysterious forces she will never fully understand—she has finally reached her highest evolution in this lifetime.

Just as a caterpillar innately seeks expansion into its butterfly form, we are likewise born with the power to evolve—indeed, we are born with the *need to grow*. Retracting, then blossoming; giving up the known to enter the unknown; surrendering what's safe and familiar to achieve our highest potential. The butterfly is well-acquainted with these secrets of the soul.

As souls, each of us chooses to incarnate under a particular astrology sign. We choose a star chart based on the things our souls most crave to learn, what we most need to heal, and what we long to experience in this unique lifetime. Soul growth astrology is the art and science of identifying these yearnings of the soul and making the most of the astrological energies that support our soul's journey through this precious incarnation on Earth.

The Earth is a kind of university, where souls come to learn. Lifetime after lifetime, you slowly develop your potential, choosing the astrological signs whose energy you most need to harness in order to grow. Soul growth astrology merely affirms your soul's deeper wisdom. Your soul sees the value in every experience you have, including hardships and setbacks, dark nights of the soul, and moments of struggle, confusion, and grief. This makes sense once you realize that, on some level, your soul *chose* these very struggles, knowing that they were necessary for your evolution.

Every astrological chart contains an infinite number of possible expressions, from the coarse to the subtle. During your journey here on Earth, you have the power to evolve the ways you express your own sign. For example, you can transform fearful manifestations of your energy into fiercely loving ones. You can polish the aspects of yourself that feel like curses, until they are revealed as the treasures they truly are. Your astrological energies are alive, pulsing, and desiring to grow with your initiative. When you approach your planets with the intention of evolving these energies, you own the fullness of your power and potential.

Reading the Signs

Before we talk about how the energies of each astrological sign can facilitate your soul's growth, let's take a look at what those energies are and how they can affect your life path. This, of course, is just a quick review of each sign. We'll cover them in more detail in the following chapters. It will help you to have your natal astrology chart handy so you can reference each planet and asteroid by sign. Here, we'll just focus on the astrological signs—without considering, for example, the twelve astrological houses or the aspects between planets—but this will help to get you started.

If you need a copy of your natal chart, there are many free resources available online, including Astro.com, Astro-seek.com, and a variety of free astrology apps you can download to your phone or other device. You'll need your birth date, birth time, and birth location in order to create an astrology chart.

Your Planets in Aries

Planets in Aries are known for being leaders, pioneers, and mavericks. Their souls desire to go their own way and express their independence with confidence. They are guided by their gut instincts to trust themselves and follow what is speaking to their energy, which tends to move quickly and enthusiastically. They are fueled by creative potential and are often the first to try something, and can be happy to show others the way forward as well. Planets in Aries love nothing more than to "get there first," plant their flag, and enjoy the experience fully—and then move on to the next adventure.

Those with Aries energies can also come across as bossy, self-involved, immature, argumentative, and impatient. In their need to move fast, they can easily forget the needs and opinions of their friends, families, and other important people in their lives. They may even lack empathy for them. The Aries soul growth journey involves maturing these lower expressions into true empathy, compassion, and understanding for those around them. Aries souls are also learning to consider the consequences of their actions before they take a leap—to understand what they are fighting for and determine if it's worth it. They are driven to examine what they are trying to prove by being the best at something, when competition is not always the best approach to every aspect of life.

Your Planets in Taurus

Planets in Taurus are determined to be secure, rooted, and creative, and are beautifully gifted with a steadiness that others find calming and reliable. They are highly capable of building lives they love, but they require stability and space in order to thrive. They desire to grow through the beauty of the physical world, and tend to seek connection through the joys of what exists in their immediate environments. The desire for financial security can compel them to work hard and invest their energy in ways that will pay off in the long term.

Yet Taurus expressions can be too self-reliant and unknowingly push people away. They may also have too much pride to ask for help or feedback. Their natural resistance to external pressures can be a strength, yet can also lead them to build up walls to keep others out. They can turn their backs on the world and shut down their life force when overwhelmed by big life changes. The Taurus soul growth journey involves trusting change when it arrives, and learning not to dig in their heels as a power move against their own personal evolution.

Your Planets in Gemini

Planets in Gemini are intelligent, curious, fast-moving, and proficient at handling many energies at once, giving them a dexterity in life that few other signs possess. They seek to talk, to explore, and to interact with their environments, keeping their fingers on the pulse of life. With their heightened ability to process a great deal of information, as well as a desire to share it, they are gifted communicators who can effectively tune in to what is essential to know and understand.

But on the flip side, Gemini expressions can be ungrounded, distracted, and unreliable, especially when their desire for stimulation crosses the threshold into over-stimulation. Planets in Gemini can be thoughtless with their communication styles, for example by gossiping just to have something to talk about. They can also be flaky, letting down those who were counting on them. Their energy can be focused in multiple places at once—to their own detriment—and they can lose sight of what is important in the long term. It is essential for them to learn to stop over-thinking, over-evaluating, over-processing, and to avoid speaking without considering the effect their words may have. They need to become more trusting of internal messages. The Gemini soul growth journey is to learn the power of words, thoughts, and messages, with an intentional focus on long-term priorities.

Your Planets in Cancer

Planets in Cancer often show up as caregivers, supportive presences, and kind allies who listen to the experiences of others with an empathetic ear. They are intuitive and emotionally wise, and can tap into the unspoken needs in a situation or relationship. They have a desire to bond emotionally and share themselves freely, and they quickly learn to be highly selective about whom they allow into their internal world and experiences. In some cases, this selectivity can look to others like protective walls or emotional barriers. Cancer expressions often learn the hard way that not everyone can be trusted and not everyone has their best interests at heart. Their softness and vulnerability can lead them to be too open and available to the harsh energies of the world. As a result, some Cancer expressions learn to close down their own needs and focus on accommodating others instead, especially if their emotions, sensitivities, and talents have not been understood or validated.

As the Cancer soul growth journey unfolds, these souls learn to avoid being defensive or hyper-sensitive to external energies. They have a tendency to shut themselves off from the world and feel an intense loneliness, which is the exact opposite of what they truly desire. It is imperative that they learn how to regulate their feelings, reactions, and emotional responses, as it can be overwhelming for them to feel so much and not know how to move the energy through consciously. They can be over-giving to the point of suffocating others with their nurturing or their desire to support. This can reveal where they need to practice greater detachment. Cancer souls are learning to "care, not carry," and to develop a clearer understanding of their powerful emotional world.

Your Planets in Leo

Planets in Leo are known for being confident, ambitious, loyal, and protective of those they love. Their big hearts "love to love." Their energy can be very generous and fun-spirited, and the desire to enjoy the best of life is a strong guiding trait in their daily actions. They can be courageous risk-takers who will go for a dream or focus on creating a life they love, especially when they can share their hard-earned possessions and adventures with others.

But their qualities of loyalty and protectiveness can become a blind spot when they refuse to acknowledge errors or mistakes, or when they hold grudges that turn into long-term resentments. Their need to accumulate success or demonstrate importance can be too ego-driven and can result in a disconnection from their hearts and from quality connections with others. Leo souls can have too much pride, or express their loyalty in ways that do not ultimately serve them. Their soul growth journey involves learning to use their leadership skills and courageous spirits with heart, as well as knowing that there is no need to compete with others when they truly love their own light and creativity.

Your Planets in Virgo

Planets in Virgo are gifted with the ability to organize, strong analytical skills, and a desire for self-improvement. This is the go-to astrological sign for synthesizing the mind-body connection in practical ways. Virgos are natural problem-solvers who can find the errors—and solutions—that can help with healing, decision-making, productive next steps, and anything that requires thoughtful discernment. Their need to be useful is a beautiful asset in both their personal and professional lives, as they become known for making things work better and more efficiently. They can also tune in to the messages of the body, and can easily discern what lifestyle habits support their daily energy and health needs.

Yet Virgo expressions need to stay mindful of when they are over-thinking to the point of stress, worry, and anxiety that directly impacts the body. Their mental energy can run rampant and be all-consuming if it is not moderated through regular physical movement and exercise. Virgo energies are learning not to be overly critical of what they perceive to be wrong or not working, as this can come across as harsh judgment and criticism. Their soul growth journey involves regulating the mind-body connection with greater consciousness and ease in order to achieve peaceful harmony and acceptance of what is, even when it is not perfect.

Your Planets in Libra

Planets in Libra are known for being social, stylish, and charismatic. They can exhibit a natural ability to talk with anyone about nearly anything. Libra energies tend to be affable and inquisitive, and to seek out interesting and enjoyable relationships. They feel energetically balanced and neutral to others, gifted with a keen listening ear and the ability to hear multiple ideas or opinions without being overly swayed by emotion. They are well-connected with people in all areas of life, and can hold their own in conversations on many topics. They often function as "middlemen" in human dynamics because they are able to navigate circumstances with grace and to make peace in situations when needed.

But at the same time, the Libra soul growth journey is about learning to avoid always doing what other people need, want, or expect. Planets in Libra must learn to prioritize their own needs and desires when considering those of others, rather than subordinating them to what they fear others may think or perceive.

Even though their awareness of other people is strong, they are learning not to compare themselves to others or to be overly focused on what others are doing or saying. They can strengthen their own sense of self by pursuing healthy connections, and by learning that it is not necessary to stay in relationships that do not honor their authenticity or give them room to assert themselves.

Your Planets in Scorpio

A passionate, investigative nature drives planets in Scorpio to learn more about the things that speak to them, especially at an intuitive level. They are curious, observant, and clever, and love to dig into the heart of a matter, while also observing the reactions and responses of others along the way. Scorpio energy can open up the magical realms of human psychology. Scorpio energies seek out intense experiences and powerful emotions as they investigate what's operating beneath the surface of their lives and relationships.

Yet the desire to accumulate more information and wisdom can become an obsession that Scorpio energies find difficult to turn off or moderate. A craving for power can lead them to take extreme measures, and adopt a no-holds-barred approach to getting what they want. They can be suspicious and untrusting, and revel in using secretive methods to obscure what they are really thinking or doing. The Scorpio soul growth journey involves learning how to come out of the shadows and maintain a sense of personal power and truth that is forthcoming and wise.

Your Planets in Sagittarius

Plantets in Sagittarius are always ready to get the party started and have a grand time in life. They are restless by nature and are known as seekers of knowledge. Their energy encourages them to broaden limited perspectives with interesting nuggets of wisdom and to focus on how to make the most of any given situation. Sagittarian energies love voyaging into the unknown, just to see what's out there that may be fascinating to explore. They are often mystical, interested in truth, and tend to form personal belief systems about the world at large, viewing their soul's greater callings in life through that lens.

When planets in Sagittarius run rampant without boundaries or empathy, however, they can manifest as judgmental or righteous. They tend to make assumptions before assessing what is right or wrong about a situation, an experience, or a viewpoint. They can be known for having strong opinions, and can create factions by taking a clear stance on controversial subjects and allowing a sense of righteousness to color conversations. The Sagittarian soul growth journey involves opening up to a variety of thoughts, opinions, and ideas without creating either divisiveness or judgment.

Your Planets in Capricorn

Planets in Capricorn are master builders of responsibility, commitment, and determination. They are grounded and seek to create worthwhile lives they can be proud of. They are often seen as ambitious, mature, and wise, and can guide others forward with a realistic understanding of what is required to get to a goal or destination. They are known for being able to handle a lot at once, especially when they are called to step forward and run the company or the family.

Yet Capricorn energies' focus on external pursuits, recognition, and productivity can lead to a hardened heart that is detached from empathy—one that forgets how to take pleasure in the everyday experiences of life that aren't connected to an achievement or goal. Capricorn souls can become too focused on work, status, and titles, leaving them working late into the night and trapped in tunnel vision in pursuit of a particular outcome. The Capricorn soul growth journey involves opening up to quality connections, as well as taking a break from the pressures of the world in order to live a more balanced life.

Your Planets in Aquarius

Planets in Aquarius are gifted with independence, intelligence, creativity, and a unique flair for connecting with the human spirit across all walks of life. Their curiosity and authenticity can open them up to myriad relationships and friendships that create a global network. They come to life when they are following a passion that inspires them to make the most of their talents in this lifetime, especially if it brings together others with the same values. Count on Aquarian energies to offer new insights, wisdom, and a higher understanding of what they perceive in the world around them.

But planets in Aquarius can also become disengaged and rebellious when life is not going their way, or they feel lost on their path. They need to attach themselves to a spark or inspiration and put their energy into it. Without that attachment, they can become disenfranchised or alienated, and this can prompt them to shut down their energy. Aquarian energies do not want to be told what to do with their skills, gifts, or talents, which can make them feel even more marginalized when they want to fit in or belong to something greater than themselves. Their soul growth journey involves accepting their unique spark, ideas, and vision as a needed contribution to the whole.

Your Planets in Pisces

The soft, loving energy of Pisces offers a kind respite from the harshness of the everyday world. Planets in Pisces are imaginative, whimsical, intuitive, and empathic, making them wonderful friends and great listeners to anyone who seeks their presence. They are often blessed with many spiritual gifts. They can tune in to the frequencies of a room, and are born with the ability to understand what is being felt or left unspoken. Pisces energy brings in beauty, harmony, and a gentle trust in life that can be reassuring on stressful days.

Yet Pisces energy can be very inconsistent and unreliable as well. Indeed, Pisces souls are well known for their "disappearing acts." Their resistance to becoming overly saturated in real-world matters can lead to strong escapist tendencies, and these are often interpreted as avoidance or lack of accountability by others. They can also seek out anything to replace the stress of modern life, which can lead to addictions or unhealthy habits that allow them to disassociate from important matters. The Pisces soul growth journey involves learning to trust their own needs, emotions, and energies on a regular basis, without avoiding their daily tasks.

How To Use This Book

Most begin their astrology adventure with a focus on their Sun sign and its attributes. However, once you begin to explore your whole astrological chart, you will quickly develop a fuller understanding of your energy—and of your soul's purpose in this lifetime.

Your five personal planets—Sun, Moon, Mercury, Venus, and Mars—comprise your personal needs, desires, actions, and thoughts. Each of them offers you opportunities to grow in significant ways that support the fullness of your potential and your life path. By looking at each of these planets in detail, you can move toward a more conscious understanding of your personality, and discover new ways to support your soul's growth.

Although you may be inclined to focus on your Sun sign, I highly recommend looking at each planet in your astrological chart. For example, your Moon sign is connected to your most personal needs and daily energy, while your Mars sign is connected to your desires and the ways you express emotions. You'll get a much more personal understanding of and insight into your chart if you consider the energies of each of these planets by their astrological signs. You can find more information on your five personal planets in my book *Awakening Astrology: Five Key Planetary Energies for Transformation.*

Start with your Sun sign, then consider your Moon, Mercury, Venus, and Mars placements. These are the most personal energies in your chart. Identify each planet by sign, and then read the chapter for that sign. For example, if your Moon is in Taurus, your Mercury is in Virgo, and your Venus is in Libra, read the chapters for each of those planets.

After examining your five personal planets, move on to Jupiter, Saturn, and Chiron, and then to Uranus, Neptune, and Pluto. Jupiter and Saturn are transpersonal planets that hold significant themes for your life path, including your blessings and your support systems, and where you have to invest more time, energy, and work. Chiron has gained prominence in astrology since its discovery in 1977, and has provided incredible insights into the soul wound you are healing in this lifetime.

The three outer planets—Uranus, Neptune, and Pluto—are associated with generational energies and the collective unconscious that we are guided to make more conscious in ourselves. This book can help you understand more of the themes, expressions, and collective frequency you embody through the energies of these outer planets. Together, these elements comprise the fullness of your energy signature—your soul's unmistakable frequency, as unique to you as your thumbprint.

In the chapters that follow, I give a detailed description of each sign's energy and share a story drawn from my own experience with actual clients to illustrate the positive and negative aspects of that energy. Then we'll examine how these energies may be affecting you as you move through your own life—in both positive and negative ways. Each chapter contains exercises that are designed to help you navigate your soul growth journey more effectively. I strongly recommend that you keep a journal as you move down this path to help you reflect on what you have learned. Each chapter ends with journal prompts that are designed to encourage that reflection.

My goal in this book is to support your beautiful, expansive growth and evolution through astrology. When you examine your astrological chart through the lens of soul growth, it can empower you in ways that may feel uncomfortable at first, but will ultimately lead you to greater peace, happiness, and self-love around the fullness of your energy.

As you journey through your chart, you may feel inspired to look at each sign with new curiosity and inspiration. Every sign has its own soul growth journey—from lower, unconscious expressions to more evolved choices. You may feel the changes in slow, progressive steps, or you may feel an instant shift, as if you have just been released from a binding cocoon that you didn't know was holding you captive. Once you emerge from that cocoon, you may experience a period of adjustment as you adapt to the feeling of having wings for the first time. You may have to learn to trust that those wings can carry you. You may feel lighter and more at ease as a result of this transformation. You may sense that you have new abilities to explore, and a freedom to go places you never could have reached before.

I hope that the insights you gain from this book set you free from any limiting vision you may have had of yourself. As you connect more deeply with your authentic self and the unique essence that no one else on the planet embodies, I trust you will feel empowered to expand your self-knowledge through the soul growth journey that is uniquely yours. Above all, I hope that you learn to trust that there is divine support for you to fly higher and farther in this lifetime.

Chapter 1

Aries Soul Growth

As the initiator of the Zodiac wheel, planets in Aries burst forth with enthusiasm, determination, and courage. Because Aries is a cardinal fire sign aligned with the energy of new growth and rebirth, Aries souls are energetically designed to lead the pack. They are never afraid to explore new paths or blaze new trails. They bring a "beginner's mind" to all of their endeavors, blithely sailing past obstacles that might slow down less confident star signs.

All of this fresh, new energy can lead Aries souls to have a strong focus on the present moment and the immediate future, while sometimes neglecting the medium- or long-term impacts of their decisions. Who has time to make a ten-year plan when there are so many exciting things happening in the next ten *minutes*? Indeed, Aries souls can sometimes have an enthusiasm that outpaces their sense of time. When they get excited about something, they want to get started *right now*, and the urge to make something happen can be overpowering. Then when the dust settles, they can find themselves with so many projects, commitments, and invitations that they can't even begin to choose between them.

Aries energy is fast-moving and drawn to immediate gratification, and Aries souls often need to work hard to cultivate patience and forbearance. Those who have dated Aries souls know how hard it can be to talk them into waiting, even just a little, instead of leaping after the next tantalizing thing that captures their attention. But they can experience tremendous growth when they cultivate the follow-through needed to match their exuberance, ensuring that they will experience the satisfaction of seeing their projects through to fruition.

In the relational realm, Aries souls are blessed with sharp intuition that allows them to trust their gut reactions, even if they haven't yet arrived at an intellectual understanding of a situation. This keen intuition makes them great leaders, as they have an uncanny ability to read the room and make decisions accordingly. They also tend to make good decisions when it comes to their friends and partners, as they can immediately perceive whether someone is trustworthy or honest and has their best interests at heart. However, the quick-moving Aries energy can also be highly reactive, bringing unnecessary drama to relationships. By slowing down and giving themselves some breathing room, Aries souls can develop their calm, responsive, and nurturing side, making the world a better place for themselves and others.

With their brilliance, determination, and willingness to forge new paths, Aries souls have tremendous gifts to offer the world. By learning to balance their need for speed with the calm steadiness required to see things through to completion, developing genuine curiosity about others' lives, and learning to manage their intense emotions, they can become the wise, steady, and courageous leaders they were born to be.

Life in the Fast Lane

Lisa is an adventurous and determined woman with bright blue eyes, a deep voice, and a contagious laugh. She's never been afraid to pursue opportunities, especially when they're related to her career. As a somatic therapist who guides people through deep-trauma release exercises, she enjoys being her own boss, and has a large client base and plenty of professional connections.

Lisa has four strong Aries placements in her natal chart and, like many Aries souls, she excels at charging ahead and going after what she wants, regardless of whether or not there's a well-trodden path to lead her there. But despite her many professional connections, Lisa has trouble sustaining quality friendships in her personal life. "I crave deeper connections with people," she said, "but somehow I never manage to turn acquaintances into real friends."

As we discussed her situation in more detail, it became clear that Lisa was very focused on herself, her world, and getting her own needs met in relationships. When I asked for a few recent examples of when she had helped someone else with a task or problem, she wrinkled her nose and asked: "Do clients count?" When I asked her about the last time she'd reached out to an acquaintance just to find out what was going on in that person's life, she came up blank.

"I guess I don't reach out to people very often, unless it's to book a session or check in about work," she said. Lisa also shared that the friends she *did* have seemed to have a hard time keeping up with her. On weekends, she craved adventure—rock climbing, mountaineering—and felt restless in low-key social situations like going to a movie or meeting up for breakfast. In fact, one of her friends had recently told her: "I feel like I'm too boring for you! But the fact is, I don't *want* to go sky-diving every time we hang out."

Although Lisa's Aries traits of self-sufficiency and ambition had served her well when it came to her career, they had caused her to neglect any human relationships that didn't immediately meet her needs or further her goals. She put energy into professional connections that could boost her career, but neglected friendship for friendship's sake. Her need for novelty and stimulation often left friends and romantic partners feeling like they weren't "enough" for her.

Lisa illustrates a classic growth need for Aries souls: truly caring about what's going on in other people's worlds, and valuing others for who they are rather than for what they can provide. Although their energy, ambition, and single-minded focus can be a tremendous gift to those around them, Aries souls can grow by learning to be caring friends and empathetic partners, and by beginning to enjoy the many gifts of deep connection. They can also learn to access the novelty and excitement they crave without leaving their loved ones in the dust or making them feel inadequate.

Embracing the Slow Lane

If you are an Aries soul, you may move faster than other people, and feel frustrated when they don't match your pace. *I sent that text message* thirty seconds *ago, and they still haven't texted me back!* You may also think faster than others, and find yourself twiddling your thumbs while you wait for the rest of the class, team, or group to catch up with you. If you've spent your whole life in the fast lane—like Lisa—it can be hard to understand why everyone else needs to move so darn slowly. But part of the Aries soul growth journey is to recognize that many of the finest things in life can only be experienced at a slower pace—including friendships and relationships with less speedy souls.

As an Aries, it's important for you to remember that not everything needs to occur on your timeline—and that's a good thing! Even when you are excited to go and ready to begin, it is a demonstration of your wisdom to trust that plans are meant to come together according to divine timing—which is not always as fast as Aries timing. Know that some things will take longer than you want them to because the Universe is co-creating with you, not dragging you back or slowing you down. When you have an expectation that moving fast is always best, you may miss some of the beautiful developments that can unfold over time.

Besides, life isn't always perfect in the fast lane, either. The desire for instant results and immediate validation can cause you to lose interest when a project hits a snag or moves too slowly. While you are probably great at starting projects, you may often struggle to see them through to completion. Once the novel, exciting parts are finished, you may become impatient and rush off to the next thing, leaving behind a trail of half-finished projects—or a trail of frustrated friends, partners, and coworkers who are left to pick up the slack. By learning to slow down and be patient, you can build a reliability that others will respect, and enjoy the rewards of seeing your projects through to fruition.

Exercise: The 10-10-10 Technique

This technique has been taught by many coaches, but was popularized by O magazine columnist Suzy Welch. It can be a useful tool for helping you expand your sense of time.

It works like this: When you are about to make a decision or take an action, pause and ask yourself how you may feel about this decision or action ten days from now. Then ask how you may feel about it ten months from now. What about ten years?

When you ask yourself these questions and write down your answers in a journal, it can help expand your perspective to include not only the present moment but the medium and long term as well. Aries souls can use this practice to get past their tendency for instant gratification, and to encourage them to consider the future impacts of their actions and decisions.

Exercise: The "What and When" Technique

Aries energy can cause you to get excited about a wide range of opportunities, and take on more projects than you truly have time to see to completion. This exercise can help you develop follow-through and avoid finding yourself in a pileup of half-finished undertakings.

The next time you feel the urgency to start a new project or take on a new responsibility, take out your journal and write down a list of exactly *what* this project or responsibility will entail. Will it involve meetings? Trainings? Deadlines? Phone calls? Physical labor?

Next, get out your calendar and figure out exactly *when* you will do all of the steps involved. Will you make the phone calls on Tuesday evening? Attend the meetings on Wednesdays? Will you have to cancel other obligations to make room for this new project? Will you still have time for relaxation, self-care, and tending your relationships?

Going through this scheduling process can give you a much-needed dose of reality and develop your ability to make wise choices. It can also help you avoid the embarrassment of taking on projects and responsibilities impulsively, only to abandon them later and let others down.

From Self-Focus to Empathy

If you have planets in Aries, you are here to have new adventures in this lifetime with the intention of getting to know yourself better through them. You may be very preoccupied with this process, constantly asking yourself: What interests me? What excites me? What do I want to be the best at? What can I do with my energy that will light me up? All this self-exploration is not a bad thing, but it can cause you to lose sight of the fact that other people's lives and experiences are just as important as your own. Your tendency to be the star of your own personal movie needs to be tempered with intentional curiosity and empathy for others.

As an Aries soul, you may feel a deep need to follow a very specific path, or to have a life that is more exciting and unconventional than others might settle for. You may feel that you have carte blanche to create the life that suits you, unconstrained by the fears, obligations, or limitations that affect others. This can lead you to do great things and live life to the fullest. At the same time, however, it can lead you to come across as self-centered or even narcissistic, placing your own needs at the center of every interaction with others. An intense focus on self can also lead you to miss out on the deep joy of being of service to others. However, when you learn to expand your focus beyond the self, you can become an empathetic friend, a caring lover, and a truly generous human being.

One of your core strengths is independence. Perhaps you've observed that you're more comfortable being on your own and following your own path than most other people in your life. But one of the downfalls of being hyper-independent is that it can lead you to think that you have to do every-thing on your own and that you cannot ask for help or guidance. It may not occur to you to invite others into your world. At the same time, your extreme self-sufficiency can be intimidating to others, and cause them to assume that you don't need or want them in your life. You may have to be very intentional about inviting others into your life, even when you don't strictly *need* to. Yes, you are totally capable of hanging up the curtain rods by yourself, but it's actually much easier to do with another person, and it gives you both an opportunity for con-nection.

Exercise: Step Back and Practice Objectivity

The next time you catch yourself getting frustrated with a friend or coworker, take a moment to take a step back mentally. How would you perceive the situ-ation if someone else were to ask you for help? How would you advise them? Once you step back and practice objectivity, you may find that your perception of the situation shifts significantly.

This simple practice can be very effective at nudging you out of a limiting self-focus, and remind you that other people also need empathy and grace.

Releasing Reactivity

Yum, that foot in the mouth tastes delicious! When Aries souls feel threatened or defensive, they can respond explosively, saying and doing things in the heat of the moment that can seriously destabilize their relationships. If this is true for you, you may feel that these outbursts are out of your control—that they some-how just happen. Because you are so connected to the present moment, you can have a tendency to expect that the people around you will simply move on after an outburst—after all, it's in the past, and you have already forgotten about it. This can leave you confused when those around you withdraw in the wake of an angry comment or petulant behavior.

Although your Aries ability to move on quickly is a good thing, you can grow when you realize that the things you say and do can have a lasting impact on the people around you—there's no "delete" button for an emotional explosion. Over time, this emotional reactivity can erode relationships, leaving you with a reputation for being a loose cannon or a hothead. Emotional reactivity can also lead you to make impulsive decisions—quitting your job, ending a relationship, or making other big moves that aren't necessarily in your best interest.

If you have planets in Aries, it may feel like your emotional energy can be unpredictable. And you're right—we can't always control how we feel! However, we are all responsible for how and when we express those emotions to others. By stopping to reflect on how your emotional reactions may impact others, you can avoid lashing out in destructive ways, and instead use your emotions as vehicles for deepening your relationships with others and practicing true vulnerability.

Exercise: Calming Reactivity

Aries souls can find it difficult to dial back their reactions in the heat of an intense interaction with others. Luckily, our digital lives offer plenty of opportunities to work with intense emotions when there's nobody else around.

The next time you get a text or email that triggers you, turn off your device and set a timer for ten minutes. While the timer is running, sit still and watch whatever your mind and body are doing. Ask yourself:

- Do I have a strong physical urge to jump up and fire an angry text back?

- Is my mind frantically rehearsing all the things I want to say?

- Do these urges remain just as intense for the entire ten minutes?

- Do these urges begin to soften the longer I sit?

- At the end of ten minutes, do I still feel inclined to say or do *exactly* what I would have done when I first got the email or text?

- Has my inclination changed?

Notice if your mind feels clearer, and if you are better able to assess a reasonable response instead of giving a knee-jerk reaction.

Exercise: Dialing Down Urgency

Your connection to the present moment can make you feel as if it's urgent to respond to people *right away*. Dialing down this false sense of urgency can be key to calming your tendency to emotional outbursts.

The next time you feel triggered by a person around you, allow yourself to notice the sense of urgency that arises. Then buy yourself time by saying something like: "I need a moment to think about what you said before I respond."

Visualize a dial like the volume knob on your car stereo, and see yourself turning this dial down until your sense of urgency goes from flaming red to an easy green.

When the urgency has abated, respond to the person in question. Notice if what you said is more calm, reasonable, and non-reactive than it would have been had you responded while your dial was still in the red zone.

Journal Prompts

Consider these questions in the context of what you now know about Aries soul growth. Record your thoughts in your journal so you can return to them as you move forward on the Zodiac wheel.

- Reflect on a time when waiting paid off in a beautiful way for you. What would you have lost if you had rushed to act, decide, or begin?

- Write down a few activities that you normally do by yourself, like walking the dog or going to the bookstore. How might it benefit you to include another person in these activities? How could it benefit the person you invite?

- Think of a time when you successfully avoided saying or doing something in haste. Looking back, do you feel relief and gratitude toward yourself for not saying or doing that thing? What would the consequences have been if you had said or done it?

Chapter 2

Taurus Soul Growth

As the second sign of the Zodiac, Taurus takes the inspirational spark of Aries and manifests it in a tangible form. Taurus souls come to Earth with a desire to settle into regular routines and habits. They work hard to establish comfort, order, and security, then maintain those conditions diligently throughout their lives. Ruled by Venus, the planet of creativity, self-worth, and finances, Taurus souls are focused on establishing predictability in an unstable world. They cannot be rushed into anything, and often require space for their decision-making process, especially if they are evaluating a long-term outcome.

Planets in Taurus have a gift for tuning in to their senses and appreciating what they find all around them—the soft, velvety texture of a rose petal, the familiar notes of a favorite song, the lingering taste of a sweet raspberry, the wafting scents of vanilla in the kitchen, the joy of a rainbow on the horizon. They connect deeply to the pleasures of their physical environments, and enjoy tending them with care. With their appreciation for beautiful things, they often have a gift for decorating and creating warm and comfortable living spaces.

Unlike other signs who may struggle to identify their goals in this lifetime, Taurus souls are often born knowing exactly what they want, and possessing the determination to keep bulldozing a path until they get it—with no compromise, no negotiation, and no giving up. Their "slow and steady wins the race" mindset makes them a force of nature. They are known for being robust, strong, and solid, and they are comfortable taking matters into their own hands. They ask practical questions and assess circumstances based on knowable facts: How much will this cost me, financially, energetically, and physically? Will it be worth it for the long term? However, their self-reliance can sometimes lead them to feel that they can never show vulnerability or accept help from others. When they open themselves up to the gifts of interdependence, they open themselves to the beautiful experience of being supported by others and held in a web of community.

With their strength, practicality, and creativity, Taurus souls have many gifts to offer the world. They come to this planet knowing exactly what they want and how to get it, and tend to avoid the over-thinking that can hold back other signs. When they learn how to thrive on change, develop their sense of security, and be vulnerable with others, they can make the most of their potential in this lifetime, charging past limitations and becoming beacons of inspiration for all they encounter.

Moving On

Kathy worked as an analyst at a financial institution for nearly twenty-two years. As a Taurus soul, she loved the stability of her job, including her simple morning routine of black coffee, one pastry, a fifteen-minute drive to work, and a brisk walk into her glass-and-brick office building, an architectural landmark in her city. She enjoyed the bright sunlight streaming into her workspace and the friendly interactions she had with many people there, connections which had grown over years of holiday parties, baby showers, and summer picnics. The money didn't hurt, either—at this point in her career, she earned a fat paycheck every month and was looking at a very comfortable retirement.

But when Kathy heard that her department was downsizing, she started to feel anxious. Upper management wasn't sharing many details about the process, and Kathy's floor buzzed with gossip and speculation. Were they going to lay off everyone in her department? Would she be moved to a different department? Would her salary be cut? Would she be able to find another job, considering the fact that she was nearing retirement age? Even though Kathy was already well-off, she still found herself obsessing over how the change might impact her financially, while giving less thought to how it would affect her friendships and her social life.

Late on a Friday afternoon, the senior human resources officer called Kathy into her office and told her she was being reassigned to another department in two weeks. Not only that, but her new department was officed in a different building in a less prestigious location. She reassured Kathy that her new position would be comparable to her current duties and responsibilities, but Kathy still felt a tide of inner resistance rising up inside her. "How can they do this?" she thought. Two weeks wasn't long enough for her to finish up her existing projects, much less absorb the shock of having to change her entire routine.

When Kathy and I discussed what she was experiencing, she expressed anxiety, frustration, and a sense of outrage. "I put so much effort into making my office exactly the way I like it," she said. "The houseplants, the photographs. I'm not even sure if my new office will get the same amount of sunlight." She also grieved the change in her routine—a slightly longer commute that took her through different neighborhoods, and different coworkers in neighboring offices. She'd been proud to tell friends and acquaintances that she worked at a famous building and felt that she would be losing prestige working at the new location. Several times over the course of our session, she circled back to financial concerns. "At least I'm not taking a pay cut," she said. "But they're going to stop matching my 401k, and that's going to have a huge effect on my retirement."

Like many Taurus souls, Kathy was laser-focused on practical concerns and on the material aspects of the change—the new office, the different commute, the reduction in retirement benefits. She liked things the way they were, and even though she was making it through the downsizing more or less unscathed, the fact that she hadn't *chosen* the changes made them unpalatable to her. Even though she was already well-off, she nevertheless felt that her security was being threatened. She would also miss the feeling of strolling up to the tall glass building that appeared on every postcard of her city and enjoying the sense of status it gave her.

As a Taurus, Kathy was used to lowering her horns and charging ahead to get things done. Feeling vulnerable was uncomfortable for her. Instead of admitting how frightened she was by the prospect of change, she focused on all the reasons why it was unreasonable. Although she had come to this lifetime blessed with strong determination, willpower, and practical skills, she now had to grow her ability to accept instability, trust in life, and build a sense of meaning and security that wasn't entirely based in money. She needed to move on.

Overcoming the Fear of Change

Taurus souls take their routines and their comfort zones very seriously. If you have planets in Taurus, you probably put a great deal of effort into building exactly the life you want, right down to the flowers on your table, the tea in your cup, and the route you take for your daily walk. This intentionality is a beautiful strength, but it can also lead you to feel a disproportionate sense of alarm when someone or something threatens to change things. Because of the strong sense of ownership you feel over the experiences of your life, you can jump to the mistaken conclusion that any and all changes that come from outside forces will be worse than what you would have chosen for yourself.

With planets in Taurus, you are blessed with strong creative and aesthetic gifts, but you can also become strongly attached to the way things look and feel. Even a simple change like neighbors painting their house a different color, or hanging a set of windchimes, or trimming the hedge to a different height may disrupt your sense of beauty and harmony. Your friends and partners probably learned early on not to rearrange the living room furniture without consulting you first! But that doesn't mean you are a control freak merely for the sake of being in control. You really do have a talent for aesthetics, and seemingly minor changes can be a major source of irritation to you.

Yet, despite having very good reasons for resisting change, you can experience tremendous soul growth when you learn to give change a chance. By resisting new experiences, you risk closing yourself off from wonderful new opportunities, including friendships, career paths, and avenues for enjoyment. You also risk unintentionally alienating the people around you when you dig in your heels and refuse to get on board with changes simply because you didn't initiate them.

When you open yourself up to the possibility that change is good, however, you give others a chance to demonstrate their talents and skills, and learn to place trust in others and in life.

Exercise: "Wouldn't It Be Wonderful?"

The next time you find yourself confronted with a change you find threatening, flip it around and pretend that it is something you were secretly longing for.

For example: "Wouldn't it be wonderful if they built a new apartment complex on my block? That would bring in so many potential clients for my dog-walking business. And it will bring more young people and families to the neighborhood, which will be so nice."

Sincerely put yourself in the mindset of a person who feels that this change is the best thing ever. Imagine that you have been hoping and praying for it for a long time.

Even if you don't fully agree with *everything* you say in your "wonderful" statements, articulating them can help you find the silver lining to the clouds that are threatening your horizon. This can help break you out of the Taurus conviction that all change is bad.

Making Peace with Money

The expression "money makes the world go 'round" may have been coined by a Taurus soul. As the first earth sign of the Zodiac, Taurus energy is strongly focused on meeting material needs. If you have planets in Taurus, you may put a lot of time and effort into acquiring houses, cars, and possessions, and the money it takes to maintain them. While other signs may be preoccupied with love or romance, you may be asking yourself: How much will this cost me? How can I get a good deal? Do I want to put more money into this? Your careful assessment of your finances is an expression of concern for your stability, your security, and your quality of life. In this sense, finances are a kind of "love language" for you.

But this interest in your finances can lead you to be hyper-focused on money, to the exclusion of other important factors required for a stable and secure life. You may check your bank balances while neglecting your relationships. Or study financial markets while ignoring your spiritual life. Because money makes you feel safe, you run the risk of becoming a miser—letting money pile up while the roof leaks and the deck rots. Or you may build a sense of security by spending your money on status symbols to reassure yourself and others of your financial success. Your Taurus appreciation for beauty can sometimes turn into a compulsive need to buy beautiful things, and can even manifest as a shopping addiction.

You can experience tremendous growth when you give money an appropriate place in your life, alongside other elements like relationships, hobbies, service activities, and spiritual practices. By recognizing that money is just *one* pillar of a secure and comfortable life, you can expand your focus to include other important aspects of safety and security. You can also grow when you recognize that money can be used to help others, not simply to satisfy your own desires for beauty, status, or comfort.

Exercise: Grounding into the Earth

Before money existed as a concept, human beings found their security in their bodies and in the Earth. Even though we now live in a highly industrialized society, our basic security still comes from the Sun, the rain, and the abundant and nourishing earth. This exercise helps you tap into that basic, physical, felt sense of security that is your birthright.

Find a pleasant, grassy spot where you can walk barefoot. Take off your shoes and stand on the grass with one hand on your belly and one on your heart. Feel the ground against your bare feet, and your breath rising and falling in your belly and chest.

Allow yourself to feel that deep roots extend through your feet, anchoring you to the Earth. Feel the energy of the Earth nourishing and supporting you. Recognize that, while the money in your bank account is an abstract number, the Earth beneath your feet is real and present, right now and always.

Exercise: Giving to Others

As a Taurus, you can evolve your relationship with money by making a practice of giving to charity every month. Choose an amount that requires a small sacrifice for you financially, whether that means giving up five dollars or five thousand. When you squeeze a little to give to the less fortunate, you affirm that love, compassion, and solidarity are more important than individual comfort.

Giving to charity also helps you remember that security is relative—there are *always* people to whom your lifestyle looks extremely comfortable and secure, no matter how precarious it may feel to you. If you feel anxious with "only" one thousand dollars in your bank account, think of the refugee to whom that money would mean the difference between life and death, or the debt-bonded workers who must earn thousands of dollars just to buy back their freedom.

When you make your monthly donation, take a moment to be grateful for all that you have, and to feel sincere benevolence for those who have less security than you enjoy.

Embracing Vulnerability

Taurus is the sign of the bull, and planets in Taurus are renowned for the strength that allows them to clear a path wherever they choose to go. If you were born with planets in Taurus, you can probably shoulder heavy loads that might overwhelm most people, and keep working toward your goals long after others have exhausted themselves or given up. This strength and determination is part of what accounts for your success, including financial success. Yet this reputation for strength can make it hard for you to admit when you're struggling or when you feel afraid, and to accept help from others. Indeed, you may have a hard time accepting even a compliment from others, let alone practical or emotional assistance.

As a Taurus soul, you may have an unconscious tendency to push away incoming streams of support, gifts, and assistance that the Universe is sending you, as this subtly threatens your sense of strength and self-sufficiency. This, in turn, can impact your relationships, because those around you may feel rebuffed in their efforts to connect with you. You may even have a reputation for being too "bull-headed" to let others into your space, and this can cause you to lose out on the emotional support you need, or the practical assistance that could make your life easier.

Taurus souls can grow by learning to see the value in vulnerability. After all, we all experience times of fear, anxiety, and sadness—so why not turn those moments into opportunities to connect, rather than burying them behind a facade of infinite strength? By getting in touch with your vulnerable side, you can improve your relationships and open yourself to receiving the gifts you may have turned down before.

Exercise: Corpse Pose

Intentionally practicing surrender can help you set aside your strength and control temporarily, and embrace total vulnerability. Who are you when you're *not* large and in charge? Can you be at peace in this vulnerable place?

If you've ever been to a yoga class, you are probably already familiar with corpse pose, or Savasana. If not, the instructions are simple. Lie flat on your back, with your feet turned outward and your palms turned upward. Remain that way for at least ten minutes.

As you lie in this position, allow yourself to sink into the experience of being a corpse—with no further responsibilities or actions to take in this lifetime. Surrender into this pose as deeply as you can.

Exercise: Accepting the Gift

If you have planets in Taurus, you may unconsciously push away help or assistance offered by others because you are more comfortable handling everything yourself. This exercise can help you expand your capacity to receive.

The next time somebody gives you a compliment, don't respond right away. Instead, take a moment to imagine that the compliment is warm sunlight falling on your skin. Allow yourself to experience the pleasure of this wonderful sensation. Let it spread through your heart and down through your whole body.

Finally, smile at the person and say "Thank you!" for making you feel so wonderful.

Sincerely accepting a compliment isn't just about making *you* feel good—it makes the giver feel wonderful to know that their gift was received, not rejected.

Journal Prompts

Consider these questions in the context of what you now know about Taurus soul growth. Record your thoughts in your journal so you can return to them as you move forward to the third sign on the Zodiac wheel.

- Recall a time when you had to accept a change, whether you liked it or not. When the change took place, was it really as bad as you feared? Did anything good come out of it that you didn't predict?

- Consider what makes you feel secure in life—besides money. Your friends? Your skills and talents? Your faith? Are you investing as much energy in these sources of security as you are in your finances?

- Think of a time when you were held or comforted by another person, whether as a child or an adult. How did it feel to surrender into that person's care? Did this experience leave you weaker, or were you nourished by it?

Chapter 3

Gemini Soul Growth

The Zodiac wheel moves into Gemini at the height of springtime in the northern hemisphere—a time of change and excitement, when flowers are blooming, seedpods are bursting open, and fresh green leaves are unfurling on the trees. Those born with planets in Gemini thrive on constant change, whether that means moving from job to job, or from relationship to relationship, or from one living situation to another. They're happiest when they're making new discoveries, setting up shop in a new place, or getting to know someone for the very first time.

Gemini is a mutable air sign. Gemini energies breeze through life and rarely get bogged down or stuck in the mud. They are ruled by Mercury, the planet of communication, and are known for their gift of gab. They are great conversationalists and storytellers, and often become writers, filmmakers, public-relations workers, or teachers. They're also keen students, and tend to go far in their education, whether that's an advanced academic degree or a prolonged apprenticeship in a skilled trade or with a master craftsperson. They are known for being extroverted and intellectual, and love to read, travel, and learn new things. Gemini souls are happiest when planning their next adventure, deciding which classes to sign up for, or hauling home a big bag of books, magazines, or graphic novels to read.

Planets in Gemini are flexible, responsive, and tuned in to subtleties of communication that may be lost on others. Their fast-moving minds can absorb a lot of information at once, processing data at a rate that might overwhelm others. If you need someone to read a dense, complicated book for you and summarize it in a few sentences, ask a Gemini! At the same time, Gemini souls often have a hard time appreciating the slower pace of other minds. Their desire for novelty and adventure can leave old friends feeling neglected as they flit off with an exciting group of new acquaintences.

Traditionally represented by twins, this sign is connected to the experience of duality. Gemini souls come to Earth seeking to understand both sides of a dynamic. Over the course of their lifetime, they may be drawn to experiencing life as a teacher and a student, a parent and a child, a business owner and an employee. They are gifted at seeing both sides of a situation, and sympathizing with both parties in a conflict. But, although this may be well-intended, it can also cause friends to question whether they are truly loyal, or just attempting to be popular with everyone. In order to achieve their soul growth potential in this lifetime, Geminis can learn to empathize sincerely with the experiences of others, practice true loyalty to those closest to them, and appreciate the gifts of commitment and depth rather than spending their whole lives chasing novelty.

Nonetheless, Gemini souls have the capacity to be loyal friends, grounded and authentic partners, and reliable coworkers. And when they develop that

needed his space, and that need for distance was most pronounced when it came to his family relationships.

In order to become the kind of parent he wanted to be, Thomas needed to slow down, open his heart to deep connection, and find ways to stay engaged, even when he wasn't in "life of the party" mode.

Managing Your Multi-tasking

I'll have one of everything! Life offers a multitude of opportunities for growth, and Gemini souls love the openness of possibilities. Geminis are natural multi-taskers who enjoy doing many things at once—hardly surprising for the sign of duality! But, if your energy prompts you to pursue lots of different opportunities at the same time, you risk stretching yourself too thin. And when you become overburdened, you may feel restless and distracted, or fail to follow through on commitments.

If you have planets in Gemini, you probably find yourself needing to correct mistakes, choices, or decisions that didn't quite pan out the first time because you weren't giving the situation your full attention. You may often miss important information because of your tendency to multi-task, because you aren't fully engaged with intention and mindfulness. When you've taken on too much, you may notice that you don't seem to be making any progress or accomplishing anything, no matter how many "do-overs" you attempt. You may even notice a pattern in your life in which one project doesn't come together, but another one does because you were approaching the second with greater focus and intention. Or perhaps the first project was a learning experience and the second presented an opportunity for growth.

The theme of duality shows up everywhere in life for Gemini souls, and remembering this can help you be more mindful of where you are focusing your energy. It can be a difficult balancing act, but as you move through life, you can learn to rise to the challenge with agility.

Exercise: One, Two, Three, Be!

Gemini souls are often so involved in *thinking* that it can take a little nudge to transition into *being*. Consciously reminding yourself to come into the present can make that process joyful and intentional rather than a drag.

The next time you find yourself feeling restless or distracted during a social interaction, call your mind back by silently reciting the phrase: "One, two, three, *be!*" As you count down, remind yourself that everything you require to be fascinated and engaged is right here, in this very moment.

When you arrive at the word "be," pretend you are seeing the world for the first time, and that everything is fresh and new. Can you find wonder and amazement in the present moment, whether or not you are moving fast?

Exercise: Visualizing Nature

Because Gemini souls come to this planet with such active minds, standard meditation advice to "just focus on your breath" can leave them feeling even more restless. Instead, try a meditation practice with a visual component when you want to relax.

Begin by sitting in a comfortable position and taking a few deep breaths to center yourself. Set a timer for five minutes. Eventually, you can work up to longer times, but it's best to start with a shorter period.

Next, choose an image that feels relaxing to you, and visualize it in as much detail as you can. For example, you might visualize the petals of a flower slowly curling inward and closing up for the night, a bank of clouds rolling in over a mountaintop, or waves crashing against a beach, one after another.

Immerse yourself in this image for the duration of your meditation. Feel yourself relaxing as you watch this beautiful natural process unfold.

At the end of five minutes, bow to yourself, and go about your day. Remember that you can return to this relaxing image whenever you like.

Cultivating Commitment

Gemini souls are like resort guests at a buffet—they're here to try a little bit of everything, and will be happy as long as they're not pressured to commit to the lobster or the steak. If you have planets in Gemini, you are probably notoriously hard to pin down, and get squirmy when others push you to agree to do a certain thing at a certain time. You will fight like crazy to avoid committing to something or someone. You will *definitely* be at your friend's baby shower next weekend— unless you're at your other friend's book launch, or your coworker's Dungeons and Dragons game, or the grand opening of the hot new restaurant in town.

You're probably a master at keeping your options open. This quality can be very helpful and protective, because it keeps you from rushing to make decisions the way some other signs do, and this can keep you from needing to backpedal if and when you change your mind. But keeping your options open only works for so long—because eventually, other people will be only too glad to close those options for you by taking them off the table. Friends may feel that you are always evaluating your choices and waiting to see if something better comes along, and they may distance themselves from you if this pattern repeats itself too many times. And worse yet, you may miss out on the many opportunities in life that are only available to those who learn how to say "yes" and mean it.

Committing to something and following through builds trust and goodwill. And when you learn the pleasure of commitment, you can grow to become a loyal and devoted friend. Sure, you may occasionally miss a more exciting event or opportunity that popped up after you said "yes" to something else, but how much does that really matter compared to the benefits of being a dependable and trustworthy friend, parent, or colleague? Although as a Gemini soul you may never quite shake your sense of FOMO—fear of missing out—you can learn to tolerate it, while embracing your commitments in the present.

Exercise: Facing FOMO

The fear of missing out can feel intense and overpowering, especially if you have planets in Gemini—even though you may not be exactly sure what it is that you're afraid of. What are you really risking by RSVPing to that wedding invitation? And what do you stand to lose if you don't?

The next time you find yourself feeling the anxiety that arises around making a commitment, pause and ask yourself: What's the very worst thing that will happen if I miss out on this event or opportunity? For example, maybe you're afraid of the sense of disappointment you'll feel when you see your friends' photos of the event on social media.

Then ask yourself: What do I stand to gain from honoring my existing commitments? For example, maybe you'll make your friend or family member happy by showing up when you said you would, and this will strengthen your relationship for many years to come.

Answering these questions truthfully can help you realize that your mind was exaggerating the possible downsides of missing out, while minimizing the benefits of honoring your commitments.

Exercise: Choosing What Is

Our minds are sometimes rebellious creatures, and when we try to make them act against their will, they can become very grumpy very fast—a fact Geminis know all too well. But when you actively *choose* whatever it is that you are doing, even if it's uncomfortable or unpleasant, you bring your mind into alignment with your will.

The next time you feel restless at a family gathering or social obligation that may not be as exciting as your other options, silently repeat the words: "I choose to be here." Then remind yourself of your reasons for attending that not-so-stimulating soccer game or baby shower. Maybe you want to support a friend, or simply follow through on a desire to be more reliable.

Simply affirming that your presence is *your choice* will help you relax into the situation and let go of your mental resistance.

Showing Your Real Face

Planets in Gemini can gain a reputation for being two-faced—not out of any conscious attempt to be duplicitous, but simply because the persona you present to the wider world may not be the same as your true self. You may be easy and breezy in public, but tend to keep your emotions to yourself. Although you may be a great communicator when it comes to telling stories and conveying information, you may struggle to speak your own truth, which can lead to confusion when you say one thing in public, then express a completely different opinion to your close friends.

The Gemini tendency to get bored quickly can feed into this pattern. In the early phases of a friendship or relationship, you may seem very interested, attracted, and engaged, only to turn into a completely different person when your boredom and restlessness inevitably catch up with you. This can leave your friends and partners feeling whiplashed when the person they thought they knew seems to disappear. However, this is often simply because you need space to process the unfolding relationship, and have a need to withdraw after the initial rush of attraction.

As a Gemini soul, you have come to Earth to learn to trust others with your true self, and to communicate your emotions, not just your great ideas and your brilliant intellect. You may find it easy to entertain others, but much harder to let them know when you need some downtime, when you're feeling overwhelmed, or when you just want to be alone for a while. However, when you get comfortable showing your true self to others, you can experience a depth of intimacy and closeness that deeply nourishes you, closing the gap between those eternal twins.

Exercise: Owning Your Feelings

Is it hard for you to differentiate between what you *really* feel, what you *want* to feel, and what you think *others* want you to feel? Sorting this out can be a simple matter of asking yourself the right questions.

The next time you feel uncertain, ask yourself:

- How do I want to feel?

- How do I think the people around me want me to feel?

- Now, how do I really feel?

By asking yourself these questions, in this order, you can distinguish between social expectations, the desire to please, and your true emotions.

Exercise: Cultivating Intimacy

True intimacy means being willing to let others see you when you're not at your sparkly, shiny best. Although as a Gemini, you may have a habit of withdrawing from others when you're tired, overwhelmed, or not completely "on," showing others your vulnerable side can deepen your connection with them rather than harming it.

The next time you feel tempted to hide your less-than-shiny face from a close friend or partner, challenge yourself to reach out instead. Spend ten or fifteen minutes talking to this person when you *don't* feel at the top of your game. Do you notice a certain sense of peace and security in trusting someone with your vulnerable self?

Journal Prompts

Consider these questions in the context of what you now know about Gemini soul growth. Record your thoughts in your journal so you can return to them as you move forward into the second quarter of the Zodiac wheel.

• Consider a time when it was easy for you to slow down—for example, spending time with an elderly grandparent you cherish and respect. What made it easy for you to give that person your full attention?

• Think of a time when someone made a commitment to you, and showed up for it—for example, a parent who was always present at important events, or a friend who passed up other opportunities in order to spend time with you. How did it feel to be valued in this way? How can you pay this gift forward in your own life?

• Recall a time when you showed your true self to a friend or loved one. What was it like to let somebody in at a deep level? How did it change that relationship going forward?

Chapter 4

Cancer Soul Growth

As the fourth sign in the Zodiac, Cancer comes onto the scene at the summer solstice in the northern hemisphere, the longest and brightest day of the year. It signals a season of berry-picking, backyard barbecues, and long, lazy days at the beach. Planets in Cancer bring a personal touch and kind-hearted energy to our everyday busy lives, and provide a much-needed relaxing vibe.

Cancer is a cardinal water sign that is ruled by the Moon. Cancer expressions are known for being deep, emotional, nurturing, and changeable. They are highly sensitive to the energies of the people around them, and are drawn to careers like nursing, teaching, psychology, and social work, in which their gifts of emotional attunement and support can make a positive difference in the lives of others. They excel at hearing what is left unsaid—the subtle undercurrents of communication that other signs sometimes miss.

However, this attunement can also earn Cancer souls a reputation for being inconsistent, emotional, and moody. They can soak up other people's energy like sponges, whether or not they mean to, and this can lead them to feel sad, stressed, or anxious without knowing why. For this reason, they must take special care to process whatever energy they are holding, especially when unwinding after a social event or coming home after a long day at work. Unlike some other signs who can party every night with no ill effects, they *need* a few quiet nights in, or even the occasional solo retreat where they can truly unwind and get in touch with themselves.

When Cancer souls are born to attuned and attentive parents, their empathic gifts develop naturally. However, when they are born to parents who do not understand their energy, they can sometimes end up suppressing their sensitivity through over-eating, over-sleeping, or zoning out with movies or on social media—a habit that can persist throughout their lives if not consciously addressed.

Cancer souls must also be conscious and intentional about cultivating self-love. Their extreme sensitivity can sometimes cause them to worry that there is something wrong with them or that they must try harder to be "normal," and these fears can only be dissolved by complete self-acceptance. Luckily, there is an ocean of love just waiting for them to find it, and no end of beautiful experiences for these kind-hearted crabs to enjoy during their time here on Earth.

When they allow that ocean of love to flow into them, even as they constantly send love out to others, they can balance their energy and thrive on their soul growth journey. Although they can sometimes seem like cantankerous crabs when others get too close, they have the potential to be deeply supported and cared for. Just as the Moon waxes and wanes, Cancer energy is in a constant state of flux. But through conscious practices, Cancer souls can ensure that these cycles remain in healthy balance, bringing peace and well-being to themselves and everyone around them.

Hard-Shelled Crab

Susan was the manager at a popular gift shop in a charming seaside town, with a warm and nurturing Cancer soul. She was the single mother of two teenagers, and the unofficial mother to many of their friends—not to mention the adoring "cat mom" to a whole gang of stray cats she fed on her back porch every evening. She was also a caregiver to her elderly father, who had moved in with the family after falling and breaking his hip. Susan's home was a safe haven, filled with comfortable couches, delicious snacks, and kind words. She loved to cook, and even after a long day at the gift shop, she whipped up a hot meal every evening, taking pleasure in the ritual of chopping, measuring, and stirring pots on the stove.

But in the swirl of caring for others, Susan often forgot to care for herself. Instead, she self-soothed by grabbing a cinnamon bun on her way to work, a caramel latte at break time, and a hot tray of fish and chips at lunch. The food was a quick reward that gave her a reliable burst of pleasure, but it could never quite make up for how depleted she felt after giving to others all day and well into the evening. As a result, she was both physically and mentally exhausted, and significantly overweight.

When it came to her relationships, Susan often slipped into codependent or even controlling behavior—hovering over her kids to make sure they didn't forget to do ordinary tasks, and being hyper-vigilant about her father's moods and health. His illness made him quite cranky, and Susan couldn't help but pick up on these emotions the second she walked through the door. She then proceeded to do everything in her power to manage her father's moods, trying to cheer him up or distract him so he wouldn't throw one of his increasingly frequent tantrums. Meanwhile, he felt patronized by Susan's behavior, and resented her attempts to help him.

Despite her warm and caring energy, Susan had a surprisingly hard shell, as I found out when she came to me for help. She had no problem telling me about the issues going on in her friends' and children's lives, but was reluctant to let me in on her own emotions. Eventually, she confided that her self-protective tendencies were one of the reasons her marriage had fallen apart. When she felt vulnerable, she backed right into her hole in the sand and nothing could make her come out. "He would try to get me to talk about how I felt," she said. "But I just couldn't! And then I got angry at him for pushing me to try."

Since her divorce, Susan had dated one other man, someone who was very sweet and doting, but whose endless problems threatened to sink her and throw her life into chaos. She finally broke off the relationship when he borrowed her car and crashed it, costing her thousands of dollars in repairs that should have gone to her daughter's college fund instead.

As a child, Susan had been very sensitive and emotional, and other children had teased her for it mercilessly. As a result, she learned to retreat when she felt threatened, and to reject others' attempts to peer beneath her shell. In typical Cancer style, her desire to connect was tempered by a fear of rejection—and when she felt hurt or overwhelmed, it could take her hours or even days to recover, despite her best efforts to move on.

Susan had to learn to balance her care for others with an equally strong current of self-care. She had to develop the ability to feel and empathize with the people around her without feeling the urgent need to solve all their problems or fix their emotions. She had to find ways to soften her hard shell when it was safe and appropriate, so that those closest to her could care for her, just as she so often cared for them. Her nourishing maternal energy could only reach its highest expression when she learned to navigate the ocean of emotion with solid boundaries instead of getting swamped by its waves.

Self-Care for Cancers

Because this sign has so much natural empathy for others, Cancer souls must be extremely intentional about building a self-care practice. Self-care means being proactive about your physical, mental, and emotional health, and using all the tools and knowledge at your disposal to ensure that you are processing stress and managing your energy appropriately. All too often, Cancer souls give and give and give, only to realize that they have become severely depleted. This depletion can manifest as physical exhaustion, emotional burnout, or even an overdrawn bank account resulting from their attempts to help anyone and everyone without considering their own needs.

If you have planets in Cancer, self-care may involve solitude. Although you may spend all day mentoring students, caring for patients, or simply brightening the day of anyone who walks through the door, you may need time alone to recharge your batteries. There is nothing a crab loves more than a solitary walk on a moonlit beach, and the same is often true for souls born under its sign. Cancer's connection to the Moon makes Cancer souls naturally nocturnal creatures. For this reason, the best time for you to practice self-care may be in the evening or even late at night.

You also have to learn to distinguish between true self-care and less-helpful self-soothing practices like binge-watching TV shows or over-eating. Although these activities may feel comforting in the moment, they often result in a temporary numbing of emotions rather than a true release of stress. Although you certainly deserve a little comfort after all of your selfless giving, it's better to take a bath, find a ball of soft, cozy yarn and do some knitting, or have a snuggle with the cat or dog, while slowly allowing your excess energy to drain away. When you recognize your own worth and care for your mind and body accordingly, you become healthier, more balanced, and less prone to energetic collapse and the addictive behaviors that go along with it.

Exercise: Scheduled Self-Care

Do you often find yourself so busy responding to the needs of others that you have no time and no energy at bedtime to care for yourself? To counteract this tendency, try scheduling your self-care, just as you would a dentist appointment or a trip to the vet.

Open your calendar and, for every day of the week, identify a time when you will engage in a self-care practice for twenty minutes. Then identify exactly which self-care practice you will do at that time, and write it down. For example: Monday, 7:00 PM, 20 minutes journaling; Tuesday, 8:00 PM, 20 minutes stretching.

Set alerts on your phone to remind yourself of the activities you've scheduled. When your reminder goes off, politely excuse yourself *even if you are helping somebody else*, and honor your commitment to yourself.

This exercise helps boost your awareness that caring for yourself is just as important as caring for others.

Exercise: Moon Ritual

Because Cancer is ruled by the Moon, you can find comfort and relaxation by creating a unique ritual that draws on the beauty and energy of this familiar friend in the night sky.

Consult a Moon calendar to identify the next full Moon. Set aside some time alone when you know the Moon will be high in the sky. When that time comes, bring a small blanket or beach towel outside.

Sitting or lying on the blanket, allow yourself to feel the Moon's beauty and radiance saturating your mind and body like a delicious bath. If you like, you can set an intention or make a wish. For example: "May I be happy; may I be at peace." Remain on your blanket for as long as feels right to you.

You can close the ritual by bowing, singing, or making whatever other gesture feels meaningful to you.

From Fixing to Empathizing

Because Cancer souls feel so much care for others when they are open and trusting, they naturally want to help people with their problems and comfort them when they're feeling sad or overwhelmed. If you have planets in Cancer, this may lead you to get overly involved, taking on friends' and family members' problems as your own, or even appointing yourself as a "rescuer" to complete strangers. Giving stranded travelers a place to stay, adopting stray animals, and dropping everything to help victims of wildfires, floods, or hurricanes are all beautiful examples of Cancer behaviors. On the other end of the spectrum, however, these behaviors can cause you to become codependent, giving up everything in a vain attempt to "help." You may smother your partner or children with an excess of intrusive "fixing" behaviors.

As a Cancer soul, you must realize that just because you have the capacity to help—in the form of time, money, energy, or other resources—doesn't mean that you automatically need to open the taps and let them flow until you're empty. Instead, ask yourself: How much can I give without becoming depleted? Will I still have something left over for all the other things I need to do? Learn to recognize when your giving will truly benefit a person who needs it, and when you are simply making yourself endlessly available to others who need to learn to stand on their own two feet.

The ocean is bottomless, and so is the capacity of those with planets in Cancer for love and care. However, your physical energy, time, and financial reserves do have limits that need to be respected. An important part of your soul growth journey is realizing that you can offer infinite love and care to people, while setting limits on what you will *do* for them. Caring doesn't have to mean dropping everything to bail someone out of an avoidable disaster, intervening in someone else's work or relationships, or helping others do things they are fully capable of doing for themselves. Instead, let your love and care manifest as a sincere and gentle wish for others to thrive, while giving them space to figure out the details for themselves.

Exercise: Tree Visualization

Do you find the urge to help and fix overwhelming? The next time you find yourself trying to sort out the problems of others or manage their emotions for them, try this brief exercise.

Take a moment to visualize a big, leafy tree. A tree can provide shade and shelter on a difficult day. But it doesn't get involved, sticking its branches into everything.

As you connect to the image of the tree, imagine yourself playing the same role for your friends, your partner, or your acquaintances. See yourself listening to them and providing comforting shade, without attempting to live their lives for them.

Exercise: Nature Observation

We can learn a lot from observing nature. Insects and animals get into difficulties all the time, but they mostly manage to sort out their own problems without human intervention. After all, when's the last time you tried to referee an argument between two birds, or interfere in the affairs of a spider?

Once a week, spend fifteen minutes in a natural setting, watching any wild insects, birds, and animals in their environment. Notice the *absence* of the usual reflex to fix or control.

The next time you find yourself feeling the impulse to fix something for another person, remember that feeling. Remind yourself that most beings are capable of working out their problems for themselves. Indeed, this is how we grow.

Softening the Shell

Click, click! Those Cancer pincers warn others to stay away when this protective crab is feeling vulnerable or overwhelmed. Although Cancer souls offer endless warmth and nourishment to others, they can also surprise them with the hardness of the shell that protects the tender bits inside. If you are one of them, you may lavish love, kindness, and care on others, while resisting invitations to reveal yourself in return. Over time, this self-protective behavior can cause those close to you to feel as if they can't really get through to you, or as if you will never return their trust.

If you have come to this lifetime with planets in Cancer, your soul's journey will most likely involve learning to soften your shell, if and when it's safe. Perhaps you had a difficult childhood that required you to become highly self-protective. Perhaps you had your heart broken in a way that made it difficult for you to trust again. Choosing the right moment to open up takes care and caution, and you don't need to show your softest and most vulnerable side to just anybody. But when you find someone who is reasonably trustworthy, it's time to take that leap and let that person into your heart.

You may be forgiven for thinking that you are stronger than others, or that you simply don't share their need for support and connection. But this belief often belies a fear that others just won't be able to care for and support you in the same way you do for them. Over time, this lack of trust becomes impossible to hide, and can cause rifts in relationships. Instead, challenge yourself to take a risk. Soften your shell and give others a chance to show up and support you. The first time you do this successfully, and realize that your friend or partner really can be a source of strength and comfort, you'll unlock a gift of trust and love that has been waiting for you your whole life.

Exercise: Can You . . . ?

If you have a hard time asking for what you need, perhaps because of a subtle assumption that others won't be able to give it, you can challenge that assumption by boldly stating an emotional need and asking somone to fill it. The next time you need love, go to your partner or a close friend and make one of the following requests:

- Can you hold me?

- Can you tell me something good about myself?

- Can I tell you about my day?

- Can you tell me everything's going to be okay?

You may be surprised to find out how responsive people can be when you ask for what you need clearly and directly.

Exercise: Armor Visualization

Everybody needs a protective shell sometimes. But if you're a Cancer soul, it can be hard to know when to let it soften. This exercise lets you practice calling up your hard shell when you need it, and letting it soften when you don't.

Visualize a suit of strong, protective armor. It may look like a shield, or like dragon wings, or like anything else you choose. Know that this sturdy protection is available to you whenever you need it.

Now practice softening that armor. Visualize it shimmering or growing fainter, or see its shiny metal turning into fuzzy wool.

Use this visualization whenever you need to soften your shell consciously to let a friend or loved one in. Know that you can always harden it again when you really need its protection.

Journal Prompts

Consider these questions in the context of what you now know about Cancer soul growth. Record your thoughts in your journal so you can return to them as you move forward on the Zodiac wheel.

- Remember a time when you truly slowed down and cared for yourself. What were the circumstances? What did you do, and how did it make you feel? What conditions made it easier for you to practice self-care?

- Identify a circumstance in which you successfully gave friends or family members the space to work through their own emotions or find their own way out of a problem they had created. What conditions made it easier for you to do this? How did it feel to realize that, although their solution may not look exactly like yours, they found a way in the end?

- Think of a time when you successfully softened your shell and let another person in. What conditions made it easy for you to do this? What was it about this person that made it feel safe? How did it feel to let yourself be loved and cared for, the same way you so often love and care for others?

Chapter 5

Leo Soul Growth

♌

Leo energy roars onto the scene, filled with charm, willpower, and a zest for life. As the second fire sign on the Zodiac wheel, Leo is ruled by the Sun, and those with planets in this sign are uniquely blessed with the ability to follow their own guiding light. Leo is a fixed sign that stays the course, allowing Leo souls to develop their creativity, leadership, and strength to their fullest potential. They are often sought after by others when it's time to take on new enterprises or explore fun possibilities. As the Lion, Leo is also connected with pride. Souls born under this sign know the value of their gifts and talents, and have no problem accepting compliments with graciousness and open hearts.

When their energy is in healthy balance, Leo souls love to see and be seen—no shrinking violets here! Their confidence is a rare gift that allows them to flourish in business and in romantic pursuits. The attention they attract brings enviable opportunities, allowing them to pursue their dreams and live life to the fullest.

Those with planets in Leo enjoy a healthy appetite for risk-taking—not to mention the courage of a lion. They lead and teach through their brave actions in the world, and others are drawn to them for this reason. Their influence grows even stronger when their sense of purpose is connected to the heart. It is the heart, in fact, which is the secret ingredient of Leo energy. When they keep an open heart, Leo souls become unstoppable and exude amazing power and strength.

Leo energies can have a gravitational pull that draws others into their world. Yet this can also bring great responsibility, as they must learn to connect authentically with the people they attract and treat them as valued friends instead of mere admirers. Their soul growth trajectory gains strength when their confidence is channeled into the service of others and of the greater good, rather than their own individual success and self-promotion.

But these proud lions may not always be receptive to anything outside of their own thoughts, perceptions, or convictions. A big part of their soul growth journey is learning to let other people in at a deep level, actively seeking out strong connections instead of trusting that they will form on their own. This can sometimes mean admitting weakness and making themselves relatable to others, instead of dazzling them with their unshakeable self-confidence. When they learn to walk among mere mortals, they can experience the pleasure of being "of the people," while maintaining the royal qualities within.

When Leo souls harness their beauty, confidence, and inner fire for a higher purpose, they can not only attract a crowd of admirers, they can make a difference in the world and forge bonds with true friends. They yearn to use their gifts for the good of others, and to develop the wisdom of their hearts to match the magnetism of their personalities. By matching the strength of a lion with the humility of a lamb, they can create a life that elevates others, while also achieving their highest goals.

Hear Me Roar!

Sheila was known for having a special spark that attracted people and opportunities into her world. As a successful real estate agent, she seemed to connect effortlessly with her clients and colleagues, handling complicated transactions with charm and grace. At the annual holiday party, she was always the most beautifully dressed and attractive person in the room, and people flocked to her just to tell her how gorgeous she was. She frequently won awards, and had even appeared on the cover of several magazines as a top agent.

But not everybody in her world was in the Sheila fan club. Her younger sister remembered all the times Sheila had gone to parties with her pretty and popular friends, while seeming bored or embarrassed by her shy little sister. Some of Sheila's coworkers privately complained that she seemed to regard them as adulation-dispensing machines, whose sole purpose in life was to celebrate the marvel that was Sheila. Not only that, but her confident style sometimes left them feeling dismissed and undervalued. And when she got angry about something? Watch out!

Sheila could tell that something was off in her relationships, but she wasn't sure why. She confided that she felt mystified as to why her sister and other important people in her life seemed frustrated with her. What was she doing wrong? "I don't get it," she complained. "I'm always helping people out; I do good work; most people seem to really like me. But the people who are supposed to be closest to me seem, well, *critical*."

She told me that, in a recent conversation, her sister had burst out: "You think you're such a good listener, but you only listen when someone's giving you a compliment or heaping you with praise. And you're always so confident when you're telling me what to do, but when's the last time you asked me what I thought about *your* life?"

I explained to Sheila that Leo energy is often so effervescent that there can be a tendency for Leos to see only "the bright side of life," including the brightness of their own selves. With their confidence and pride, even the most well-meaning Leos can end up inadvertently dominating their relationships, leaving little room for others to feel heard or seen. Sheila delighted in sharing her gifts with others, but she often failed to realize when she was doing too much basking in her own glow. Not only that, but she had an unconscious expectation that the people around her were there to receive whatever she had to give—whether that was a funny story, a piece of advice, or an angry rant—and she often forgot that they had their own wants and needs.

The more we spoke, the more Sheila realized that she'd become accustomed to treating people like admirers rather than friends. Because she was so successful, she unconsciously placed herself on a plane above the people around her, assuming that her thoughts and opinions were naturally more valuable than theirs, and expecting them to be grateful for the advice she dispensed—or just for being graced with her presence at all. What she saw as "giving" to others could come across as preening. And the confident way she moved through the world could be seen as an affront to those whose circumstances in life had led them to be more cautious and uncertain.

As a Leo, Sheila was blessed with self-assurance and a deep trust in her own strengths. Her blazing inner fire was a valuable resource when it came to getting things done and navigating tricky terrain in her career. But this fire could also get out of control when she didn't have enough fuel to feed it. More than once, she had caught her assistant's eyes glazing over when she ranted about a difficult client, and she'd tried hard to soften her self-righteous tone, but to no avail. As for her relationship with her sister, she found it difficult to connect with someone who was so quiet and plain, and didn't seem to share her own pleasure in going to parties and being seen.

Sheila had a lot to roar about—her magnetic personality, her sincere wish to help others succeed. Her soul growth journey involved expanding her ability to relate to others on a deep level, seeing beyond appearances, and taming the anger that flared up when she didn't proactively manage her Leo energy in healthy ways.

Balancing Confidence with Humility

Need a lesson in confidence? Call in the Leo planets for examples of what it means to be poised, assertive, and self-assured. Like lions casually strolling across the savannah, Leo souls have a natural confidence that leaves a powerful impression on others, making it look as if they have everything under control. Their confidence can uplift and energize the people around them, mobilizing them around a common goal and increasing their chances of achieving it.

Yet there can be such a thing as too much confidence. If your planets in Leo are out of balance, you can come across as boastful, ego-inflated, and hard to work with. In some cases, you can become so proud and self-involved that even your most ardent friends and admirers have no choice but to back away. And in the event that you are wrong about something, your extreme confidence can make it hard for others to feel sympathetic.

As a Leo, your high level of confidence can also make it difficult for you to develop close relationships. In some cases, people may feel overshadowed or insecure around you because of it. Or they may feel that their valid concerns and insights are constantly being dismissed, swept aside by you. This can lead them to feel as if they aren't being heard, and that their plans and opinions don't matter to you.

To activate your soul growth potential, you have to cultivate humility—owning your faults, apologizing to others when appropriate, and acknowledging your mistakes. But don't worry—being humble doesn't mean lurking in the shadows or giving up the admiration of others. On the contrary, vulnerability, authenticity, and humility make you even *more* attractive. Having the confidence to show your weak side can garner even more admiration over the long term.

Exercise: Sharing Credit

One soul-expanding way to practice humility is by making a habit of sharing credit with others when you have a big win. Basking in your own glory feels great, but it feels even better when you have company.

The next time you knock it out of the ballpark at work, at school, or in your creative life, take a moment to think about all the people who contributed to your success, however indirectly. When you talk about this success with others, shift the focus from your own prowess, and expand the conversation to include all the people without whom you couldn't have succeeded. Call them out on social media to make sure they get their fair share of the credit, or acknowledge them in some other way.

When you channel some of your tremendous Leo confidence into talking up the skills and talents of others, you provide a heartfelt service to your less-visible friends, letting them know how much you value them and notice all that they do.

Exercise: Deep Listening

What's that beautiful sound? If you're a Leo, it may be the sound of your own voice. You *do* have wonderful ideas and plenty of good things to say, but you can also unintentionally take up all the airtime, leaving less assertive friends or colleagues feeling frustrated that they didn't get a chance to speak.

One beautiful way for Leos to practice humility is by seeking the counsel of others, and listening deeply to their input. The next time you're feeling super confident about a project or decision, ask three friends or colleagues for their perspective on the situation. Be sure to let them speak, instead of filling the space with your own ideas. Then repeat back what you heard them say, and tell them what you value about their opinion.

Even if you move forward exactly as you originally envisioned, humbly seeking advice can help your friends or colleagues feel like trusted confidantes whose opinions you respect, instead of mere admirers or sycophants.

Moving Beyond Appearances

When Leo souls saunter into a room, it's hard not to stare. They have fabulous personal style. They love to dress well and groom themselves with care. They see a quality haircut as a necessary expense, on a par with groceries and electricity. They are often drawn to careers like acting and modeling. Not only are they comfortable being seen and admired, they can feel as if something's wrong if people don't pay enough attention to them, or heap compliments and praise on them.

If you have planets in Leo, this innate sense of beauty and dignity is something to treasure, but beware of letting yourself be defined by your appearance, or gauging your self-worth by the number of stares, compliments, or "likes" you receive each day. Your worth as a person isn't rooted solely in your appearance, your style, or your charm, but in the purity of your heart—and that's only visible on the inside.

Your strong appreciation of appearances can sometimes lead you to surround yourself with attractive acquaintances rather than close, trustworthy, and intimate friends. When you expand your focus to include the qualities of the heart, you begin to befriend a wider range of people whom you appreciate for both their outer *and* inner beauty. One of your soul's great gifts is the ability to appreciate praise and compliments sincerely—a skill that some other signs find difficult to develop. To experience the most soul growth in this lifetime, focus on building your character and living in accordance with your values. This will ensure that you don't spend your lifetime competing with the Goodyear blimp for maximum visibility at any cost.

Exercise: Going Incognito

You may spend a lot of time thinking about how you're going to look—at a party, in a photograph, or when giving a presentation—and this can take up much more of your "mental budget" than you realize. Attention that's going into appearances is attention that's *not* going into other considerations.

Try attending a long-awaited party, or concert, or public event incognito. Instead of doing your hair, dressing to the nines, and making a big splash, imagine that you slip into the room unnoticed and strike up conversations with others instead of expecting them to flock to you.

How does it feel to *not* be perfectly dressed or coiffed? Do you feel more anxious and vulnerable? Or is it a little bit liberating? Which aspects of your personality are free to come out when you're not busy projecting a highly attractive image?

Exercise: Positive Affirmations

Beauty fades over time, and even the most attractive Leo souls will eventually have to contend with wrinkles, graying hair, and a perceived dimming of their irresistible glow. If you've placed too much of your self-worth in your appearance, these changes can cause panic. But you can grow by establishing an unshakeable sense of self-worth independent of your physical self.

Start by saying the following positive affirmations every morning shortly after you wake up. Standing in front of the mirror, and looking into your own eyes, make the following statements:

- "I am completely worthy of love."

- "I am as beautiful as the day I was born."

- "I love myself completely."

By repeating these affirmations every day, you can get in touch with yourself at a soul level, moving far beyond the surface level of appearances and into the deeper layers of your inner beauty.

From Roaring with Anger to Purring with Pleasure

Anger is a normal emotion that everybody feels from time to time. Anger by itself is not "bad" or "wrong." For instance, it can be a healthy response to an unfair situation or a boundary violation. In fact, its presence gives us valuable information about when our personal limits have been crossed. But for Leo souls, anger can be intense and fiery, and they must take special care to express their anger in appropriate ways. When Leo souls are angry, their roar can be heard three counties away!

If you have planets in Leo, their fixed nature can make it hard for you to let go and move on after you've become angry—especially if you see this as a form of giving up, showing weakness, or letting someone else "win." As a result, you can get stuck in an angry mindset, replaying past outrages in an infinite loop, and wearing out the friends, colleagues, and family members who have to listen to you rant again and again. You may even develop a reputation as a hothead who goes to battle unnecessarily, then holds grudges for far too long.

You can shift this pattern by reconnecting to pleasure and play. Like a young lion frolicking on the savannah, you are wired for enjoyment, and a good play session can defuse your stress, reduce feelings of aggression, and affirm those all-important social bonds. Play can help you move your energy in a healthy way, and remind you that there are more important things than winning. Anger and play cannot coexist in the same place. Although the energy of aggression may be present at first, play softens it and ultimately transforms it into joy.

Exercise: Burning Energy

Leo souls are born with a great deal of energy that needs to be burned up in healthy ways so it doesn't turn into pent-up aggression. Leo is a fire sign, after all. If you are a Leo soul, you can avoid angry flare-ups and keep yourself on an even keel by identifying healthy ways to burn your excess energy.

Every day, spend thirty minutes burning energy in a way that feels cathartic to you—dancing to your favorite music, playing an intense game of basketball, cycling home from work, or even splitting wood in the yard.

If you can turn this into a social activity, even better. When you burn energy with others, you form closer bonds with them, and enjoy the resulting rush of endorphins as a group.

Exercise: Choosing Your Battles

Leo anger is often triggered by a sense of unfairness. Why did *I* get a parking ticket and *you* didn't? Why did the bouncer let *that* person go backstage after the concert, but not *me*? This sense of righteous indignation can easily trigger you into a lengthy rant that changes nothing and serves nobody.

But if you practice accepting the small injustices of life, you can learn to channel your energy into fighting the injustices that really matter. When you choose your battles wisely, you can channel your Leo energy in healthy directions.

Start by asking yourself what things in life are really worth getting angry about. The fact that you got a smaller piece of pie than your cousin? Or the fact that some people in your community don't have access to healthcare? Then channel your energy into addressing the real injustice. This may mean showing up for community meetings, volunteering, or directly serving others.

By focusing your Leo energy on things that really matter, you can become a force for good in the world, while experiencing less aggravation in your day-to-day life.

Journal Prompts

Consider these questions in the context of what you now know about Leo soul growth. Record your thoughts in your journal so you can return to them as you move on to the sixth sign on the Zodiac wheel.

- Consider a person you see as a positive example of humility—perhaps a colleague who works hard while shirking the spotlight, or a spiritual teacher who chooses to live simply and declines to take credit for their accomplishments. How does humility benefit them? How does their humility serve as a gift to everyone around them? Has their humility been a limitation in their careers or relationships, or has it actually helped them succeed?

- Recall a time when you were preoccupied with some aspect of your appearance. Did it really hold you back as much as you feared? Most of us have some physical feature that isn't quite "perfect," and yet we still manage to make friends, fall in love, advance in our careers, and follow our dreams.

◆ Think of a situation when you stayed angry for a long time. What changed for you when you finally let that anger go? Did the letting go happen spontaneously, or did you have to work at it? What shifts in perception enabled you to make this change?

Chapter 6

Virgo Soul Growth

Virgo, the sixth sign in the Zodiac, is often represented as a goddess of agriculture, providing security and nourishment on the material plane. With their practical mindset and methodical style, people with planets in Virgo excel at finding step-by-step solutions for even the most complicated problems. They have a gift for always knowing what needs to be done next, and a knack for taming the chaos of daily life by breaking it down into manageable chunks. The strengths of this mutable earth sign really come alive when its energy is directed toward a worthwhile endeavor that fulfills a desire to be useful and of service. Everything—from the home to the office to the social club—seems to run better when Virgo energy is present, because it brings an efficiency and precision to tasks that others often lack. Virgo souls can quickly identify how to improve on systems and streamline processes, making life easier for everyone around them.

Planets in Virgo are highly capable and can manage a lot, but they have a low tolerance for unnecessary drama, chaos, and nonsense. If you want to indulge in a good, long gossip session or throw yourself a pity party, don't invite a Virgo! Indeed, rather than sympathy, you're more likely to get a thorough rundown of what you could have done better, whether you ask for it or not. Virgo souls' practical, analytical natures make them very valuable as friends, but their tendency to analyze can also make them seem overly intellectual or even critical.

Virgos come to Earth with a gift for detail. Planning a last-minute backpacking trip? They will want to know all the details before jumping in the car—from the length of the trail to the ingredients in the freeze-dried camp food. They excel at solving puzzles, completing their taxes error-free, and appreciating the subtleties of color and sound that make beautiful art and music. But, while this focus on detail can give them a unique window on the world, they can sometimes get lost in it, forgetting the big picture. They may get hung up on minor setbacks or zero in on inconsequential flaws, losing sight of the fact that these things hardly matter in the greater scheme of life.

The Virgo soul growth journey challenges them to be adaptable to life's unexpected circumstances, without expecting everything to proceed in a straight line or fit into a convenient container. Their evolution entails exploring what life is like outside the narrow confines of perfectionism and learning to embrace the beautiful messiness of life. After all, even when the clean, folded laundry is expertly arranged by category, color, and size, the family dog is apt to come along and sit on it or push it off the couch entirely.

With their remarkable abilities to coach and support the people around them, Virgo souls make invaluable friends, partners, and coworkers. When their intellectual and analytical gifts are balanced by self-love and emotional connection, they can thrive, enjoying deep and rewarding relationships, and excelling in their careers. Even if the world isn't as perfect as they would like it to be if they were in charge, it's still a beautiful place—and some of that beauty comes from its imperfection. By embracing that glorious and poignant imperfection, Virgo souls can find a deep sense of security and belonging, drawing closer to others and accepting themselves as well.

Mr. Perfect

Malakai was a tall and handsome Virgo gifted with a strong analytical mind and keen discernment that made him a powerhouse at work. Outside of the office, his friends often asked him for guidance when they needed to negotiate a raise, make a significant investment, or even just build a new deck. He listened patiently to whatever they had to say, then offered detailed commentary and advice on the situation at hand. Thanks to his fine attention to detail, he could often point out considerations that others had overlooked, saving them hours of time and piles of money.

When it came to his family, however, Malakai's talent for constructive criticism wasn't always such a boon. His oldest son felt that his father was always hovering over him to discover ways he was messing up. Even when his son made it clear that he wasn't looking for feedback, Malakai had a hard time restraining himself, especially when he thought he could save his son from making a mistake or doing unnecessary work.

Like many Virgos, Malakai was a perfectionist, and had a hard time relating to people who didn't share these tendencies. If it was *possible* to do it perfectly, it ought to be done perfectly—at least, that's how Malakai lived his life. He was baffled by people who didn't take the time to organize their tools perfectly, who submitted documents with typos in them, or who allowed themselves to get out of shape as they moved into middle age. Unfortunately, he was also baffled by his son, who was an Aries and prone to flitting from project to project, leaving so many things undone.

Malakai obsessed over the details of his relationship with his son. "Just this morning, I asked him to clean up his baseball gear, and he just left it in the hall. And that English assignment he was going to turn in without a cover page—don't get me started. I tried to tell him how important it is to practice professionalism from an early age, even in high school, but would he listen? He's *such* a bright kid, but he won't get very far if he doesn't start paying attention to those little details."

As a Virgo soul, Malakai prized order and harmony, and found it distressing when things were crooked, sloppy, or out of place. And like many Virgos, his keen intellect was both a blessing and a curse. He had a tremendous ability to help others, yet frequently had to restrain himself when they weren't ready or willing to receive his help. Even though, at its core, his relationship with his son was close and loving, he could get wrapped up in day-to-day squabbles, seeing them as signs of impending doom. But on the rare occasion when he took a step back and looked at his life from a higher vantage point, he marveled at just how perfect it really was.

Releasing Perfectionism

Virgo souls are drawn to perfection in any form—whether that's a perfectly shaped seashell, a sauce that comes out just right, or clean dishes neatly arranged on the shelves. This love of order and harmony is a beautiful thing, but sometimes it can lead to unhealthy expectations, especially in the realms of work, relationships, and body image. If you have planets in Virgo, you may work hard to achieve your idea of perfection, only to be inordinately frustrated when somebody else comes along and messes things up. This can leave your friends and family feeling as if they're not good enough, or even superfluous.

In some cases, this quest for perfection can focus on the physical body, leading you to obsess over diets and exercise routines, and causing you to cast a critical eye on every wrinkle, gray hair, and stretch mark. Although Virgo energy isn't known for vanity, you may set a high standard for yourself and expect to achieve it every time. This perfectionism can make you intimidating to others, who perceive you as being effortlessly flawless, not knowing how hard you strive for that image. You may be quite finicky about what you view as "good enough," and may constantly tweak things to make them better. This can sometimes leave your friends and coworkers exhausted, especially when they've met their own "good enough" threshold hours or days before.

If you have planets in Virgo, one of your tasks in this lifetime is to get a little more comfortable with chaos. That doesn't mean turning into a slob, but it does mean reminding yourself what's really important in a given situation. Does it matter that the napkins at the dinner party are perfectly folded? Or is it more important that your guests talk and laugh and have a great time? Does it matter that your child got a B instead of an A+ on their science project? Or is it more important that they truly engaged with the ideas they were studying? With a little courage, even the most fastidious Virgo souls can learn to enjoy life's ragged edges. So don't hold yourself above and apart from imperfection. Learn to embrace it.

Exercise: Tiny Failures

Your desire for perfection can sometimes mask a fear of failure. Perhaps you were criticized as a child, and sought perfection as a way of avoiding future criticism. Or maybe you've gotten so used to people thinking that you're always on the ball that you're afraid of letting them down. Whatever the reason, you can grow by giving yourself permission to fail. This exercise can help.

At least once a week, make a point of doing something you know won't come out perfectly. Cook dinner without a recipe, fiddle with a device that isn't working properly, or have a conversation with a difficult relative or neighbor.

Notice your emotions. How does it feel to take a small risk?

Notice how much you learn from these experiences—sometimes more than you might have learned if you'd stuck to something safe that you could do perfectly!

Exercise: Unconditional Self-Love

Does your pursuit of perfection sometimes leave you feeling as if you are never good enough? Over time, this can lead to a state of exhaustion and even depression. Your soul growth challenge is to learn to cultivate self-love. Indeed, that is one of the main reasons you came to Earth. Self-love can invalidate the metrics that indicate that you are only worthy when you meet or exceed a certain standard. It can also keep you from unconsciously holding others to that same standard, which can lead to strained relationships with friends and loved ones.

Practice tacking on the phrase "I will love you just the same" to any thought or command you direct toward yourself. For example, when you find yourself thinking that you really need to apply for a promotion, mentally add: "But even if you don't, I will love you just the same." If you find yourself thinking that you shouldn't sleep in for so long, try adding: "But even if you do, I'll love you just the same."

When you think those words, pause and summon the energy of love into your body. Feel yourself completely beloved in your present state, without changing anything or achieving anything.

Softening Criticism

Want some constructive criticism? How about some friendly feedback? If you hang out with a Virgo, you're likely to get both. Virgo souls are highly analytical, and when they perceive a way to make things better, it's hard for them to resist the urge to share these insights with those involved. And while others may sometimes be grateful for the free advice, especially when it saves them from making costly mistakes or doing unnecessary work, sometimes this constructive criticism can leave them feeling henpecked, misunderstood, or simply annoyed. If you have planets in Virgo, you have to learn to test the waters and make sure your feedback is welcome, lest you intrude where you're not wanted.

Your Virgo energy can probably also benefit from developing a clearer insight into the situations and people around you. Although the feedback you give may be factually accurate and well-intentioned, you may sometimes fail to consider the context—or for that matter, may blurt out advice and opinions before you understand the context at all. When offering advice, ask yourself: Do I have the whole story? Or am I making assumptions? By taking a little extra time to "read the room" and assess things like body language and energy levels, you can deliver your insights with kindness and tact, and increase the likelihood that your messages will be received well.

In your love life, your ability to analyze your partner's problems and offer helpful suggestions can be a great gift. People know they can count on you to think of reasonable solutions to seemingly overwhelming problems, and this quality can make you a source of stability in relationships. At the same time, you may sometimes come across as unsympathetic, especially when you conclude that someone's problems can be traced back to you. To grow beyond this, learn to pay attention to what your partner is *really* asking for—to be presented with a solution, or maybe just some much-needed warmth and affection. When you realize that you are valued, not only for the practical advice and feedback you can give, but also for the love you share, it can transform the trajectory of your life.

Exercise: Heart First

As a Virgo soul, you may feel dominated by your intellect, with your heart sometimes playing second fiddle to your mind. This exercise can help you create a balance between your heart and mind by encouraging you to be intentional about giving your heart a chance to lead.

The next time you feel called on to analyze a situation and offer constructive criticism, try giving love instead. For example, if your daughter comes to you in tears about a breakup, try to set aside your instincts to provide an assessment of what went wrong for a moment, and simply console her.

You can even mentally say the words "heart first" to remind yourself to tune in to the emotional quality of a situation before analyzing it intellectually. With practice, you can slowly bring more balance between your mind and your heart.

Exercise: Appreciating What Is

Your knack for perceiving how to improve things can lead you to a kind of mental and sometimes physical restlessness. While others are enjoying the view or savoring the salad, you may be thinking about how to cut down that pine tree sticking up in the middle of the fence, or wondering if there's some dill in the cupboard. But you can experience wonderful soul growth when you make an intentional practice of appreciating the way things are *right now*, without changing or "improving" them.

Every day, set a timer for five minutes, then sit still and let yourself appreciate things exactly as they are. This may mean sitting at your kitchen table, listening to the birds chirp outside the window and noticing how pretty the light is on the dirty dishes. Or sitting on a park bench, realizing it's okay that the bench is a little damp and could have been designed more ergonomically.

By intentionally falling in love with reality just as it is, with all its flaws and foibles, you can save yourself from always living in an imaginary future in which things have finally been improved, and enjoy the beauty of the now.

Seeing the Forest for the Trees

Fine-tuning, editing, correcting—these are what Virgo souls are all about. When they put "must be detail-oriented" on a job description, they have a Virgo in mind. If you came to Earth as a Virgo, you can probably catch a typo from fifty miles away, and you never drop a stitch in your knitting. You are blessed with a microscopic lens that allows you to dot every "i" and cross every "t," making you well-suited for a career as a lawyer, an accountant, or a copyeditor. Your fine eye, nose, and ear for detail can also mean that you have a deep appreciation for music, art, and cooking that may lead you to excel in those creative fields.

But the Virgo focus on detail can sometimes lead you to forget about the big picture—the garden in which that perfect rose is growing, or the feast at which your exquisitely spiced dish will be served. You need to remember the *reason* for all those details, even as you may also delight in them for their own sake. Keeping things in context can help you avoid getting caught up in obsessive behavior, losing hours or days to details that really won't matter in the long run.

Keeping an eye on the big picture can also improve your relationships. Yes, you paid for coffee this morning, but he'll pay for the subway fare this evening—things have a tendency to balance themselves out. Although you may be tempted to take a careful accounting of every little transaction, whether financial or emotional, this can lead to unnecessary stress, as the day-to-day fluctuations look more significant than they do if you look at them month to month or even year to year. By learning to value the forest as much as the trees, you can expand your capacity to enjoy life, while worrying less and feeling secure in the ultimate balance of life.

Exercise: What's the Forest?

Virgo souls can feel a disproportionate sense of stress when the details of a plan are different from what they envisioned, while forgetting to assess how much it really matters.

The next time you feel stressed by an unexpected expense, a surprise wrinkle, or an annoying delay, ask yourself: "What's the forest?" Will this obstacle or delay really throw off the whole project? Or will you hardly remember it at all? Will this expense cripple you financially? Or can you absorb it by making moderate adjustments here and there?

By consciously reminding yourself of the forest, you can feel more secure and at peace among the trees in your day-to-day life, and extend that sense of peace to those around you.

Exercise: Ditch the Plan

Do you struggle with spontaneity? After all, if you don't know all the details of an event, how will you know if you're going to like it, or if you'll be prepared? This focus on details can lead you to excessively control your life, and cause you to miss out on some of the beauty that can come from not knowing exactly what's going to happen next.

To balance out this tendency, make a point of accepting last-minute invitations. Go to that concert that starts in twenty minutes, even if you get there late and haven't eaten dinner yet. Tag along to your neighbor's party, even if you don't know who's going to be there. Notice how things tend to just work out, even if you don't micromanage every detail in advance.

Journal Prompts

Consider these questions in the context of what you now know about Virgo soul growth. Record your thoughts in your journal so you can return to them as you approach the midpoint on the Zodiac wheel.

- Make a list of the three people you admire most in the world. What qualities make them admirable to you? Their "perfection"? Their generosity? Their creativity? Their selfless-ness? Then make a list of three people who love and admire you. Do they love you because you do everything perfectly, or for some other reason?

• Consider how you can tell when others truly want feedback, and when they just want to be loved. Ask yourself how *you* feel when you share warmth and affection, as opposed to when you help someone out with an intellectual analysis or practical advice. Is there room for both strategies in your life?

• Think about what really matters to you in a job or relationship. Write down any major themes that come to mind—for example: fairness, adventure, purpose. Even if at times certain situations at your job feel unfair, or certain moments in your family life feel boring, are those relationships fulfilling your values in a larger sense, month to month and year to year?

Chapter 7

Libra Soul Growth

Libra occupies the midpoint of the astrological year—a fitting place for a sign represented by a set of scales. Planets in Libra are all about interacting, sharing, and equal exchange, which makes them gifted at connecting with just about anyone who crosses their path. Because this is a cardinal air sign, planets in Libra are gifted conversationalists who can draw out even the shiest dinner party guest, or get to know the life story of someone they've just met. With the value they place on harmony and balance, they make great diplomats, tactful negotiators, and deep listeners. They tend to be drawn to fields like psychology, politics, and public relations. Their ability to instill calm and goodwill into tense circumstances is unparalleled, and they have a knack for bringing even the stickiest situations to a positive resolution.

Not surprisingly, people with planets in Libra place a high value on their social relationships. They do not end relationships on a whim, and often go to great lengths to preserve them—sometimes putting in more energy than they really should. They may still be friends with their elementary school classmates, the coworkers from their first job, and every neighbor they've ever had. Libras would have a hard time shaking off friends and acquaintances even if they wanted to!

With their keen observational powers, Libra souls can see both sides of a problem or issue, and are experts at playing devil's advocate. However, this ability to weigh every option can cause them to be indecisive, and this can gain them a reputation for being wishy-washy. Indecisiveness can cause them to spin their wheels, never taking a firm stand or asserting themselves one way or the other. Their ability to see things from many angles, combined with their yearning for harmony, can also mean that they hang back from asserting themselves in relationships, preferring to keep the peace rather than arriving at a truly fair or ideal situation.

To their friends and families, Libra expressions offer a safe refuge from the chaos of life. They often act as the reliable "glue" that holds a group of friends or a family unit together. They are skilled at bridging differences, resolving conflicts, and seeing the best in everyone. But this responsibility can weigh heavily on them, making them feel as if they need to resolve every argument or act as middleman in every negotiation. Their soul growth journey involves tuning in to their own wants and needs, learning how to let others solve their own problems, and holding others accountable for their own behavior.

The Libra gift for forging and maintaining relationships is a boon to everyone around them, and most Libras have no trouble finding guests to attend their birthday party, their retirement celebration, or their wedding. In fact, the real challenge will probably be finding enough chairs! They can grow when they pay a little more attention to their own needs in relationships, instead of always following their instinct to make others comfortable at all costs. By allowing others to carry their fair share of the load in relationships, asserting their values, and shedding unnecessary comparisons, Libra souls can enjoy the adventure of life on this planet, while growing to meet their full potential.

Mr. Congeniality

Mathieu was an affable and diplomatic Libra who'd been voted Mr. Congeniality by his dormmates in college. Friends, acquaintances, and even strangers often came to him with their problems, knowing they would find a caring presence and a sympathetic ear. He could make just about anybody feel seen and understood, which is probably what drew him into a career as a therapist. At the clinic where he worked, he enjoyed the weekly meetings with his fellow therapists, in which everyone went over their cases and gave and received advice. Even though some of his colleagues were sometimes a little overbearing or even off-base in their advice-giving during these sessions, Mathieu kept his friendly smile and took it in stride.

But lurking behind Mathieu's congeniality was a deep-seated need to avoid conflict and make peace at all costs. As a child, he'd learned to walk on eggshells around his mother, who was a challenging woman with narcissistic tendencies. He became an expert at reading her moods, cheering her up, and distracting her from anything that could set her off on one of her rages. As an adult, he still found himself slipping into hyper-vigilance, constantly looking for ways to manage the emotions of those around him, whether they needed him to do so or not.

At the same time, Mathieu was constantly comparing himself to others, starting with his older brother, who had always been their mother's favorite. His brother had an advanced degree in psychology, and was now a tenured professor and the author of several books. Mathieu had stopped at a master's degree and gone into clinical practice. He often wondered if he should go back to school and get a doctorate like his brother. But, although he frequently weighed the pros and cons of this, he never seemed to arrive at a firm decision.

When he came to me, Mathieu seemed strangely drained and sad. "Everyone at work thinks I'm their best friend," he said. "Even the people I don't like at all! Meanwhile, I don't really feel like I have any friends at work." The cognitive dissonance between his colleagues' rosy vision of their relationships with him and his own lived experience of those relationships reminded him of his mother. "It's just like with Mom," he said. "I worked so hard to give her this *experience* of a wonderful relationship, but it wasn't wonderful for me at all. You'd think a therapist like me would have overcome his own issues by now, but I guess I'm just not as good as my brother."

Like many Libras, Mathieu was highly perceptive and attuned to other people's needs—to the point of forgetting his own. He got so focused on maintaining harmony in social relationships that he rarely stopped to ask himself if he even wanted to be in those relationships at all. He gave others the impression of peace and friendship even when they were trampling all over him. Rather than asserting himself, he acquiesced to their harmful behavior, then found a way to work around the damage in private. When he did think of himself, it was usually in the context of a comparison with others, not as a sincere assessment of his own happiness and direction in life. He often ended up "balancing the scales" out of habit, rather than for a positive purpose.

In order to find true happiness and enduring balance in his life, Mathieu needed to learn to use his Libra energy with intention and purpose, instead of letting his peacemaking talents get hijacked by anyone and everyone, to his own detriment.

Balancing the Scales

If you have planets in Libra, you probably thrive on social exchange with a wide range of people—from friends and coworkers, to neighbors and teammates, to fellow hobby enthusiasts. Your empathetic, friendly, and helpful nature wins others over effortlessly. And you probably maintain your relationships for a long time once they've been established. Your Libra instinct leads you to sympathize with everyone, and you may even emphasize the parts of your own personality that are most similar to those of others in an effort to make them feel seen and understood. In your quest to "balance the scales," however, you may come to place a higher value on *resolving* issues than on finding actual balance in the situation at hand.

As you seek to resolve imbalances in social relationships, it is easy for you to lose sight of the fact that you are doing far more than others to achieve your goal. You may dedicate a level of time, effort, and emotional investment to solving conflicts that others don't reciprocate. Ultimately, this can lead to you feeling as if you are propping up your relationships single-handedly. Or you may find yourself with a large number of relationships that would simply collapse if you stopped putting in all the effort.

Your Libra energy is drawn to harmony, and you are skilled at conflict resolution. But sometimes, what you perceive as "resolution" may involve letting someone else off the hook for bad behavior, or accepting an unfair situation— not truly resolving anything. You may rely too heavily on self-sacrifice, while depriving others of the opportunity to take responsibility for their own part of a transaction. Over time, this pattern of giving too much can leave you feeling exhausted, confused, and withdrawn. To truly balance the scales, you need to expand your focus to include your own wants and needs, not just those of the people around you.

Exercise: Just Say "No"

Do you have a hard time saying "no" to people, especially when it comes to acting as diplomat or middleman? Do you fear that your family or friend group will devolve into tribal warfare if you're not there to keep the peace and balance things out? Try taking a small risk and see what happens when you opt out of playing this role.

The next time you feel drawn into the role of peacekeeper for your friends or family, try responding with one of the following phrases:

- "Sorry, I'm not going to get involved this time."

- "I think I'm going to sit this one out."

- "You two are both great people, and I know you can work this out on your own."

What happens when you let the people around you resolve their own dilemmas? Is it really as bad as you feared? Or do you find that others really can find balance on their own?

Exercise: Building Bridges

Planets in Libra are blessed with great social skills, and this can lead you to assign yourself the task of "bridging the gap" with others without even thinking about it—especially with difficult people. And once you've given yourself that role, it can be hard to relinquish it. This can cause you to "carry" a relationship for years or even an entire lifetime. Try letting someone else put in their fair share of the effort to build those bridges.

Think of a difficult person with whom you put in a great deal of effort to make the interaction go smoothly. For example, maybe you always think up activities and conversational topics that will engage your mom, while she almost never does the same for you.

The next time you interact with this person, leave some open space where you would normally try to bridge the gap. What happens? Does the other person start putting in a little more of the effort? Do you get to put in a little less effort? How does it feel to allow someone else to build those bridges for you?

Self-Assertion Is Self-Love

Libra souls instinctively want to keep the peace, both inside themselves and in their relationships with others. But life isn't all smooth sailing, and there are always situations that call for a little disruption. With planets in Libra, you may want to sneak out the back door when strong emotions get stirred up, or when confrontations become necessary. But achieving your soul growth potential entails being decisive, sticking around, and getting comfortable with the discomfort of asserting your own wants and needs.

Assertiveness can take many forms. In relationships, it means setting clear boundaries with others, refusing to cover up for their bad behavior, and refusing to agree to terms that are unacceptable just to keep the peace. Internally, it means being clear about what you really value in life and deciding to take action accordingly, even if this involves making hard choices that have many pros and cons.

Your Libra tendency to avoid inner and outer conflict can lead you to turn into a fence-sitter, forever going over your options while more decisive signs forge ahead to achieve their goals.

Being assertive doesn't mean that you need to engage in yelling matches or make spur-of-the-moment decisions you'll later regret. You can grow in self-assertiveness by stating your own needs simply and clearly, and declining to shift your boundaries. This often means getting comfortable with letting people down, or allowing tension to exist instead of rushing in to resolve it. For many Libras, this is no easy feat! But learning to be assertive will reward you with an enhanced sense of self, and help you realize that you are just as worthy of having your needs met as those around you.

Besides, as a naturally gifted communicator, you may even be surprised at how well others hear you and understand what you need, without it dissolving into your imagined worst-case scenario. And when it comes to making decisions, you may be amazed at how much satisfaction you find in staking a claim and choosing a direction, even with all the potential downsides—much more than if you just sat on that fence for the rest of your life!

Exercise: Setting Boundaries

You may find yourself attempting to keep the peace at the expense of your own comfort, energy reserves, and peace of mind. In this exercise, I invite you to let others share in the responsibility for keeping the peace by respecting your boundaries.

Practice saying the following phrases when you're *not* actively engaged in a conflict or confrontation. Becoming comfortable with them when you're not feeling stressed or pressured can make it much easier to use them when you are.

- "I'm sorry, but that's not going to work for me."

- "I hear that you want _____, but I'm not available to give it."

- "I hear that you're feeling _____, but that doesn't make it okay to talk to me that way."

As a peacemaking Libra, you may feel anxiety when setting boundaries. But, with practice, you'll discover that this creates a healthier interaction both for you and for the other parties involved.

Exercise: Getting Off the Fence

Cutting through Libra indecision means being clear about your values and goals. After all, how can you jump off that fence if you're not sure what you're jumping *toward*?

Make a list of what you really want and value in a given situation. Be as precise as possible. For example, if you're choosing between two jobs:

- Do you want to make more money?

- Do you want a shorter commute?

- Do you want the opportunity to be mentored by more advanced coworkers?

◆ Do you want to make a positive difference in the world?

Now ask yourself which of the two jobs fulfills these goals more robustly. Once you've identified the winning candidate, go for it—and don't look back.

Moving Past Comparison

Because your Libra energy is gifted with the ability to weigh both sides of a situation, you can slip into the habit of making comparisons, especially when it comes to measuring yourself against others. Don't get me wrong—those scales can often come in handy! But when you're putting *yourself* on a scale, you can end up feeling inadequate and uncertain, constantly wondering if you're "supposed" to be living somebody else's life.

The expression "Don't compare your inside to somebody else's outside" should be every Libra's mantra. When you try to compare yourself to others, you actually have very little idea what you're comparing yourself *to*. Maybe they had an extraordinarily privileged childhood, and their path to success was paved with opportunities and resources that were unavailable to you. Maybe their seemingly effortless beauty and success belies the roiling self-hatred or depression they carry deep within. Maybe they have a career you envy, but their relationships are a mess. The point is, when you compare yourself to something imaginary, the results will also be imaginary. In fact, it's very difficult to get a complete enough picture of anyone else's life to make meaningful comparisons.

Libra souls tend to be outwardly focused, and this is a beautiful thing. But to accomplish your soul growth potential in this lifetime, you have to become more self-aware. You have to put more energy into focusing inward. Ask yourself how you are doing, independent of any comparisons with others. If you're happy in your job, your relationships, or your creative life, why does it matter how or what anyone else is doing? Learning to dig deeply into yourself and appreciate your own unique journey will not only make you happier, it will give you a deep sense of peace that will be palpable to those around you.

Exercise: Focusing In

Libra souls can pay so much attention to the people around them that they lose track of their own feelings, both emotional and physical. Try taking a few minutes to focus solely on your *own* experience.

Find a quiet place to sit where you won't be interrupted and set a timer for ten minutes.

For the next ten minutes, just pay attention to how *you* feel in your body and mind. Are you tired? Hungry? Sore? Excited? Energized? Eager to socialize? Ready to withdraw?

By working with this practice every day, you can find a balance between tracking other people's states of being, and becoming more aware of your own.

Exercise: Dropping Comparisions

Libra energies may assume that their scales are accurate—all the time. But when it comes to comparing yourself with others, this is rarely the case.

Try visualizing a big set of scales, with yourself on one side. The next time you catch yourself comparing yourself to another person, imagine a big purple question mark sitting on the other side of the scale. Remind yourself that you actually have *no idea* what you're comparing yourself to.

Repeat this practice until it becomes second nature, and the instinct to compare yourself to others will fade away.

Journal Prompts

Consider these questions in the context of what you now know about Libra soul growth. Record your thoughts in your journal so you can return to them as you move forward on your journey around the second half of the Zodiac wheel.

- Identify a relationship that feels unbalanced to you. How would you like this relationship to work? What would happen if you withdrew from it entirely? Do you *need* to keep this relationship going, or can you give yourself permission to let it go?

- Recall a time when you asserted yourself, at the risk of displeasing someone. Did it really shatter the peace as badly as you feared? Or did it win you more respect, including self-respect? Did it result in a more balanced outcome?

- Consider those you admire greatly. When you think about them, do you compare them to others? *Yes, but they aren't as rich as so-and-so. Sure, but they didn't win that award.* Consider whether you appreciate them in their own right, then ask yourself what it would be like if you treated yourself the same way.

Chapter 8

Scorpio Soul Growth

Scorpio expressions arrive on Earth with a deep need to understand who they are and what they can offer that others will love, accept, and appreciate. They are deeply intuitive , and have a gift for seeing beyond the veil of the material world and tapping into energetic realms. For this reason, they are often drawn to be healers and artists, or to follow spiritual paths. Because Scorpio is the fixed water sign of the Zodiac, its energy is intense, passionate, and emotional. Those with planets in Scorpio are deeply in touch with their emotions, to the point that they can sometimes feel things a little *too* intensely and shut down to process their internal world.

With a lot of intensity at their disposal, Scorpios can handle many situations in life that require ongoing strength and power. They are often the ones to whom others turn to express their deepest thoughts and experiences, but they can also be secretive, withdrawn, and suspicious of people's intentions until they demonstrate they are trustworthy and reliable. Scorpio souls can be experts at hiding their own intentions and desires until they're satisfied that others are worthy of their trust.

The Scorpio soul growth trajectory involves learning to trust what they feel, sense, and perceive *before* they receive validation from others, or even *without* receiving that validation. They must learn to trust their own gut instincts, rather than relying on the reactions of others. For example, if you have planets in Scorpio, you may have a strong sense that someone at work is lying, but push it aside because nobody else appears to have the same concerns. Then four months later, you hear that this person embezzled money from the company, and that the instinct you ignored was right.

Scorpio soul growth also involves learning to manage intense emotions. Because they can so easily pick up on other people's energy, Scorpios can become drained or overwhelmed by social situations. They also have a tendency to confuse others' emotions for their own, or to take on others' feelings unnecessarily. An important task for them during this lifetime is to learn to distinguish clearly what is "theirs" in relationships and social situations.

Scorpio placements often feel like they signed up for a more intense life than other signs, but they also come to this path blessed with the ability to handle it. They are here to trust their own instincts as they level up and regenerate throughout their lives, with their intuition guiding them. Their journeys tend to feature several distinct "chapters," each written as they absorb one lesson and move on to the next. They are eager to learn—and to share the gifts of that learning with others. By getting comfortable with their unique abilities, they can make a real difference in the lives of those around them, while fulfilling their own deepest desires.

Planets in Scorpio are intense, intuitive, and watery, and their task is to learn how to manage those powerful energies in this lifetime. With their deep connection to the Divine, they can act as channels to realms that other signs have difficulty accessing. When they learn to be honest with themselves and show up as who they truly are, they can forge a strong alliance with the Universe to produce truly amazing results. By stepping into their power, redefining success, and harnessing their intense emotional energy for good, Scorpios can become invaluable healers, guides, and wisdom-keepers for their communities.

All or Nothing

Jill was a talented healer and Reiki master who worked with clients from all over the world. She was a deeply attuned Scorpio who loved hosting retreats and gatherings, and meeting other people who shared her love of energy healing and intuitive work. She was fiercely competitive and found satisfaction in her growing popularity as an energy healer. She enjoyed watching her online classes and in-person retreats fill up quickly. At the same time, she was plagued with crippling self-doubt, a remnant of a childhood with a highly critical and rejecting mother. And while she was committed to her work, she often found herself flooded with emotions that she didn't quite know how to manage.

Jill had been the highly sensitive, emotional, and perceptive only child of two distracted and career-focused parents. From a young age, she experienced psychic and empathic abilities, and was keenly attuned to people's energy, intentions, and emotions. The flood of information could sometimes be overwhelming. As her skills developed, she occasionally tried to share her experiences with her mother, in a bid for support or guidance. But her mother was uncomfortable with the things her daughter revealed to her, and throughout Jill's teenage years, she slowly pushed her away.

Because of her mother's response, Jill learned to keep her abilities hidden, and even came to doubt their existence. For a long time, she didn't feel safe opening up to others about her gifts, let alone building a life around sharing them. At first, she followed the typical path of going to school and getting a corporate job, hiding her passion for energy work and healing modalities. But after several years of living this false life, she had a startling insight—she hated this version of herself! It was not her truth or her power; it did not resonate with her desires or her gifts.

In true Scorpio fashion, Jill was an all-or-nothing person. So she spent a weekend processing her emotions, then sent an email to her boss on Monday morning saying she was leaving the company, effective that day. But even as she reveled in her transition to living her truth as a healer, she knew she had to find ways to keep her highly competitive Scorpio energy from distracting her from her true values and leading her down a path of competition for competition's sake.

Like many Scorpios, Jill had signed up for an intense journey of deeply trusting herself through life, a journey that had started in childhood. So she had to find ways to heal the wounds of her past. Although she could perceive very personal details about others, she tended to be highly secretive when it came to herself, and resisted letting others get close to her for fear that they might reject her as her mother had. When she felt strong emotions, they could knock her flat, and she sometimes envied people who seemed to be able to stay on an even keel through any storm. At the same time, she knew that she'd been blessed with special gifts, and that she was being guided through life by benevolent forces. She felt her Scorpio soul had a direct line to the Divine, and was determined to use it for good.

Living Your Truth

If you have planets in Scorpio, your life journey may include an early experience of deception, perhaps by a parent, sibling, or family member who wasn't trustworthy. When Scorpio energy is young and impressionable, these experiences can lead to forming a belief that lies and deception are a normal and acceptable part of human life. This can make you perfectly comfortable with keeping secrets, altering details in the name of protecting the people involved, or even inventing stories out of whole cloth when it serves a worthy goal. What they don't know can't hurt them, right? Or can it?

Over time, these seemingly inconsequential bendings of the truth can lead you to larger patterns of deception and dishonesty, especially if you have not suffered consequences for previous lapses. Although you may start out by obscuring the truth for "good" reasons, you may end up losing track of the truth completely, living a life that feels more and more like a lie (and not a little white one!). You risk developing a reputation for being secretive. And trying to push past this veil of secrecy to the "real" you can wear out your friends and partners.

If you have Scorpio placements, you can experience massive soul growth when you get comfortable living your truth, even if it means giving up your social standing, or changing careers, or taking some other risk. Although you may feel safe living behind a veneer of social acceptability, you will only step into your true power when you let others see you for who you really are. Telling the truth in all domains of life will also make life easier, as you develop more authentic relationships and choose a path that truly resonates with your desires and abilities. When you embrace truth-telling, you can become a force to be reckoned with!

Exercise: Fessing Up

As a Scorpio soul, you may be in the habit of hiding your true self from others—whether that means being vague about your past, or obscuring your true preferences when it comes to music, food, or art. But when you take a small risk by showing someone a previously hidden aspect of your true self, you can begin to break that pattern.

The next time you spend time with friends or acquaintances, make a point of sharing something they didn't know about you. For example, reveal that you were adopted, or that you love dancing to electronic music. Your revelation doesn't have to be deep and dark. For Scorpios, even "fessing up" to enjoying black velvet cupcakes can feel like enough of a risk.

Notice if your relationship feels closer and stronger now that you've shared some previously hidden element of yourself. How does it feel to share your truth?

Exercise: Practicing Authenticity

For some Scorpio souls, the tendency to build a false front can become so ingrained that they completely lose sight of who they really are, let alone how to share that with someone else. This exercise can help you practice authenticity in a safe and anonymous setting.

Find an internet forum about a subject that interests you—gardening, astrology, or anything in between. Create an account with a screen name that does not reveal your real name or location.

Engage in conversations as your true self. Say what you really think, and share what you really like. How does it feel to show up as your true self when the stakes are low?

By practicing authenticity in a "safe" domain, you can discover the joy and freedom of speaking as your true self, and build up the courage to do so in your real life as well.

Yours, Mine, or Ours?

If you have planets in Scorpio, you're probably highly attuned to your own energy and to the energy of those around you. You may even have a hard time telling which is which. Are *you* feeling sad, or are you just picking up on your mom's emotions? Are *you* anxious, or is it just that you can tell your coworker is worried about how the meeting is going to go? Because you are so conscious of the energy of a room, you may sometimes end up feeling so drained and overwhelmed that you need to binge-watch a TV series or two just to recharge your batteries.

In other cases, you may feel your own emotions so strongly that you can overwhelm others with your intense expressions. Your friends probably don't have to stand around guessing how you feel. When a Scorpio is sad, stressed, or overjoyed, everybody knows it. And unless you carefully develop the skills to handle intense emotions, you run the risk of wearing out your friends and family with dramatic displays and exhausting expressions.

Scorpio souls tend to experience intense emotions from a young age. Sometimes these waves of emotion are too much to handle, and you have to find ways to tune them out. But as you grow into your Scorpio power, you can learn to move through these roiling waves consciously, without draining yourself or the people around you.

Your Scorpio soul growth journey involves learning to work with your emotions skillfully, so that what was once overwhelming turns into a source of nourishment and power. Emotions can be seen as "energy in motion," and thinking about them in this way can help you detach from your seemingly overpowering feelings, and see yourself as a beautiful vessel of moving energy. After all, you are not your sadness, your anger, your excitement, or your worry—you're just the container through which these energies flow.

Exercise: Personal Energy Shield

If you are a highly empathic Scorpio, you may feel defenseless against the waves of energy that other people constantly throw off. This can lead you to withdraw from social situations, or to be very careful about those you let into your circle. By visualizing a personal "energy shield," you can enter social situations without getting your batteries drained by the energy swirling around you.

Start by visualizing your energy shield in detail. What color is it? What is it made of? Does it surround you like a bubble? Do you hold it in front of you like the shield of a medieval knight? Then visualize what the energy looks like on your side of the shield. Is your own energy soft and flowing? Is it hard and chaotic? What color is it? What does it feel like to you?

When you come into contact with another person, call up this shield. Notice the difference between the energy on your side of it, and the energy on the other side. Know that your shield can hold the line between your energy and the other person's, without allowing anything unwanted to pass.

Invoke your personal energy shield whenever you need help distinguishing your energy from someone else's, or when you need to hold an energetic boundary in a social situation.

Exercise: Riding the Waves

The next time you experience an intense emotion, whether your own or somebody else's, drop any stories you may be telling yourself about that emotion. Instead, try to experience the emotion as pure energy.

For example, if you pick up a wave of intense sadness, tune out your thoughts and tune in to your body. Where is the sadness located? What is it doing? How does it feel on an energetic level?

Notice if tuning in to the wave on an energetic level helps it pass more smoothly and easily than if you engage it with thoughts and stories. Are intense emotions hard to handle in and of themselves? Or is it only the stories we attach to them that make them so?

Letting True Intention Lead

There is no mistaking the Scorpio drive to succeed. Once Scorpio souls set their sights on a goal, they will drop everything else to achieve it. And if there's competition to be had, they will revel in it, always eager to test their skills against those of others. If you are blessed with Scorpio energy, you are highly motivated to do your best, get ahead, and see how you stack up to others who are pursuing similar goals.

At a deeper level, this competitive streak may be connected to a desire to rack up successes as a way of making up for areas of life in which you've had to sacrifice. For example, you may have had a difficult childhood, but may feel that being number one in your career can make up for it. Your challenge is to recognize when healthy competition turns into jealousy, envy, or the desire to knock a rival off their pedestal just for the sake of it.

If you have planets in Scorpio, your soul growth journey involves taking a close look at the root beliefs that are driving these competitive tendencies. For example, do you have an unconscious belief in lack and scarcity? Do you think that if someone else is successful that somehow makes you less successful? Do you have an unconscious conviction that you are not worthy of receiving what you desire? Do you feel that you have to fight like hell for what you want and can't trust anyone else to support you?

When you understand the reasons for your competitive nature, you can shift from competition for competition's sake to letting your true intention and values lead. Is winning at all costs a core value for you? Or do you value quality work, whether or not you get recognized as number one? Do you really care about making the most sales in your department this quarter, or is family time a higher priority? When you let your values lead, your competitive nature comes into healthy balance, bringing about true success.

Exercise: Redefining Winning

You may have unconsciously adopted a narrow definition of success—who makes the most money, who lands the most deals, or who gets the most recognition. By broadening your definition of success, you can step off the competition treadmill and enjoy life, whether or not you always "win."

Make a list of the values you believe are important to living a good life. For example, living sustainably, serving others, or being a trustworthy presence for your friends and family.

Every day, make a point of doing one thing that directly relates to cultivating these values, even if it does nothing to further your career or bring you a typical sense of "success."

How does it feel to put more energy into living your values, as opposed to collecting wins? Does your definition of winning begin to change?

Exercise: Noticing Abundance

The Scorpio competitive spirit is sometimes grounded in early experiences of scarcity and lack. Indeed, part of the reason you chose to come to Earth as a Scorpio soul may be to heal wounds around scarcity, and move into a mindset of abundance.

Every day, make a point of noticing abundance in whatever form it manifests. This can be as simple as noticing how many clean socks you have in your drawer after laundry day, or as complex as taking a thorough inventory of your finances and realizing that you have more than most people who are alive on this planet today.

The more you notice abundance, the more you will begin to live from an abundant mindset, realizing that there really is enough to go around. Although you may still enjoy competition, it will spring from a place of true appreciation, not because you *need* to claim all the resources for yourself before somebody else snatches them away.

Journal Prompts

Consider these questions in the context of what you now know about Scorpio soul growth. Record your thoughts in your journal so you can return to them as you move on to the next sign on the Zodiac wheel.

- Recall the last time you truly felt like yourself. Were you alone, or with another person? What factors made it safe for you to show up in your truth? How would your life be different if you could live from that space all the time?

- Remember a time when you successfully held a healthy boundary around somebody else's energy. What did it feel like to notice those emotions without letting them color your world? Were you better able to be present for that person when you weren't surfing an emotional wave? How did it feel to watch those waves break from your place on the shore?

- Ask yourself which wins really matter. When you look back over your life, what moments make you the proudest? When you won the Top Salesperson award for your company? Or when you helped a child confront a bully? How can you put more of your energy into cultivating this second type of win?

Chapter 9

Sagittarius Soul Growth

Sagittarian souls arrive in the world with an abundance of optimism and ideal-ism, and are here to make the world a better place. They are never satisfied with the status quo. They are movers and shakers, looking for ways to right wrongs and eliminate injustice. Because Sagittarius is a mutable fire sign, planets in this sign prefer mobility, spontaneity, and the freedom to roam, rather than sticking to plans and schedules that are set in stone. This mutability can leave them with a wealth of stories to share—and the more exaggeration, the better the tale!

Impatience pumps through the veins of Sagittarians, and these placements are often pulsing with a sense of "what's next?" and "where can I go from here?" This tendency to move from one goal to another keeps their energy flowing, but it can also lead them to feel restless and even reckless when it is not channeled properly. They want to be free and open to whatever comes their way, and this can be perceived as a tendency to be non-committal and even opportunistic, as if they are always waiting for "the next big thing." Some even develop a reputation for being ungrounded, especially if they bump around from job to job or show no consistency in their daily endeavors.

The wanderlust spirit that makes Sagittarian planets so intriguing can cause their friends and partners to question whether or not they're truly responsible. After being drawn in by their fascinating tales, others can end up wishing they would settle down and become the solid partners or providers they wanted. Yet planets in Sagittarius are also graced by luck and good spirits, so it can appear as if they always land on their feet and that situations turn out in their favor, no matter what.

Life is a spiritual adventure for awakened Sagittarian souls. Many are shaped by the religions or spiritual practices in which they were brought up, and which continue to provide a system for understanding the world. Beliefs they gained in childhood cause them to form strong opinions and judgments about what is good and bad, right and wrong. Some stick to one belief system for most of their lives, while others move through many ideologies, philosophies, and spiritualities as part of their natural inclination to expand their knowledge base and test what is most accurate for them.

Sagittarian expressions are guided by a sense of justice, and they are often drawn to careers in law, non-profit administration, or providing direct aid to the oppressed. They may also have come to Earth with the goal of correcting errors and evolving out of lower mindsets left over from past lives. As their energy evolves, they move into a greater acceptance of differences, learning to detach from harsh judgments and rigid opinions, and begin to see the world as the vast and diverse place it is. Many cultivate this inspiration through education, publishing, travel, sacred studies, mystery schools, spiritually based teaching, or anything else that fulfills their need for continual growth.

The fiery Sagittarian spirit is here to right wrongs, take on meaningful battles, and find the lighter side of life's hardest moments. While others may turn a blind eye, Sagittarian souls never flinch from the truth of the world, and that courage carries them through countless adventures. By growing empathy for their less-fiery friends and opening themselves to vulnerability, they come to realize that sometimes it's okay to just be an average Joe. And this is how they can complete their soul's mission in this lifetime and realize their full potential on Earth.

Beware the High Horse

Shannon was a bright-eyed and idealistic twenty-seven-year-old with her eyes on the world—and a fiery Sagittarian. She had just graduated from law school, and was getting ready to find her dream job at an animal-rights organization. A committed vegetarian since the age of sixteen, she was eager to put her legal skills to work on behalf of furry, feathered, or scaly creatures both big and small. But before getting a job, she planned a six-month trip backpacking through Thailand, Vietnam, Laos, and Cambodia on her own.

Although her three older siblings were all highly responsible planners, Shannon took more of a seat-of-the-pants approach to life. Instead of reading travel guides and planning a route, she intended to buy a plane ticket to which-ever country on her list was cheapest, make friends at a backpacker's hostel, and wing it from there. Between college and law school, she'd taken a trip to India and Nepal using this approach, and had had a series of unforgettable adventures—meeting yogis in secluded mountain caves, living in an ashram for a month, and volunteering on a vegan permaculture farm. Even when she ran into difficulties—like the time she forgot her passport in a taxi in Calcutta—Shannon always seemed to land on her feet. This trait evoked her friends' admiration—and sometimes their envy.

Shannon's sister had once erupted in frustration after hearing about one of her many adventures. "It's not fair," she said. "You never plan ahead or commit to anything, but somehow you still get everything you want. Well, some people aren't so lucky."

But what her sister didn't know was that underneath Shannon's funny and self-deprecating tales about her gaffes as a traveler was a strong thread of shame and self-judgment. Sure, she could tell a hilarious story about the time she got food poisoning on the train, but at the time, she'd been mortified. Her gift for entertaining others, combined with her panache, her talkative nature, and her strong opinions, sometimes gave people the false impression that she was invulnerable. But she was really just as sensitive as the rest of us. It's just that her fiery Sagittarian exterior made that hard for others to see.

Shannon came to me just before departing on her backpacking trip. When I asked if any of her friends from law school were planning to join her for the adventure, she laughed and said: "No. It's so easy to make friends while traveling that it's actually more fun to set out alone."

She paused before continuing. "To be honest, a big reason I'm going on the trip is to get the whole law school thing out of my system. I had kind of a falling out with my classmates, and I'm looking forward to meeting people who actually care about what's going on in the world."

Shannon explained that everything had changed during the last election cycle, when she tried hard to inform her classmates of "the facts" and give them deep probing insights to consider. When I asked her for more information, she launched into a highly energized rant: "People are soooo wrong," she claimed. "They are going to look like fools, and I told them this. They sound so ignorant when they talk. I can't even stand to be in the same room when people are discussing certain topics, because they clearly don't understand what's really happening."

Yup. That level of self-righteousness is how you lose friends.

It was clear to me why Shannon's classmates had severed connections with her. She had a way of speaking that literally shut down conversations. I understood that, although she meant well, she had a tendency to get on her high horse when it came to her ideologies and opinions. Most people just wanted to see her get on that horse and ride away—permanently. It was exhausting to be on the receiving end of her extreme opinions and be pummeled by her overwhelming communication style.

Like many Sagittarian souls, Shannon was fueled by a strong sense of justice, which can be a great gift in certain circumstances. She was well-informed about world events, and truly cared about the plight of others. Where she struggled was in educating those around her without alienating them. In her rush to educate people about the "right" way to live and think and be, she unwittingly offended them. Moreover, she sometimes failed to empathize with others, and didn't try to understand *why* they made choices and had opinions that differed from hers.

Shannon needed to learn how to manage her sense of urgency when communicating her opinions. She needed to make space for the people around her to think and exist. Only by softening her rigidity and tendency to judge could she pave the way to true dialogue instead of one-sided harangues. But as an evolved Sagittarian soul, she could create opportunities to live her values, and elevate others as well.

Holding Compassion with Perspective

If you have planets in Sagittarius, you probably get all fired up about the topics that interest you, especially if they have to do with making the world a better place. As a result, you can quickly become the "expert" on subjects ranging from economic injustice to climate change. People may seek you out for your opinions, knowing that you've done the deep dives required to back them up.

But your ability to form and communicate strong ideals can be a double-edged sword, as you may have little patience with people who haven't done as much research as you have, or given as much rigorous thought to subjects that you deem important. In situations like these, you may find yourself slipping into monologue mode, drowning others in information instead of engaging them in a two-sided conversation. It's important for you to notice when the powerful urge to instruct others arises, and ask yourself: Am I truly listening to what others have to say, or am I just intent on "fixing" their wrong thinking?

If you have planets in Saggitarius, an important part of your soul growth journey consists of recognizing that every single person on the planet has their own perspective, shaped by their unique life experiences. Not everyone has had access to the same resources that you have—whether financial, educational, social, or emotional. Instead of judging others for having a "less evolved" perspective than you have, you can grow by seeking to understand them. Is your mom "wrong" for watching all that "bad TV," or is it the only way she knows how to unwind after her long day at work? Are your coworkers "thoughtless" for eating foods you consider harmful, or are they doing the best they can on a limited budget? Your challenge is to learn how to hold compassion for the people around you, even as you seek to elevate them to your level.

Your Sagittarian instinct to instruct, condemn, judge, or persuade others to change can be almost unbearably strong. But it's important not to judge yourself for having this reflex. With patience, you can learn to make space around this sense of urgency, without needing to fix everyone else's reactions—as well as your own.

Exercise: Dialing Back Urgency

The next time you feel an urgent need to "correct" somebody on opinions, or even a factual error, use creative visualization to help you choose an appropriate energy level with which to communicate.

Imagine you're driving a big, heavy bus down the highway. If you slam on the brakes to avoid a hazard, everyone on the bus will be thrown forward in a way that may frighten or injure them. But by dialing back the urgency of the situation—by signaling, pulling over, and coasting to a stop—you can address the problem without negatively impacting the passengers on the bus.

Dialing back the urgency of your exchanges with others doesn't mean biting your tongue or suppressing your knowledge, however. It just means being mindful of the experience of those around you, and taking them into consideration when you communicate what you know.

Use your visualization any time you want to slow yourself down and communicate more gently, instead of rushing to correct or instruct others.

Exercise: Broadening Your Perspective

Your Sagittarian soul growth journey involves broadening your perspective. Try spending five minutes every day considering another point of view that may seem foreign or unusual to you—a person with different political views, a sensitive news story, or even a deep belief you have held your whole life. Ask yourself:

- ◆ What strengths might this ideology, opinion, or belief have?

- ◆ In what ways might this worldview make sense?

After five minutes, make a wish for this person (or situation) to be healthy and free from suffering. Wish the same for yourself as well.

Embracing the Everyday

Sagittarian souls have a tendency to make bold declarations, and will never let the truth get in the way of a good story. *The doctor said it was the worst concussion she'd ever seen! The fish was this big! They said I was the only American who'd ever completed the World's Spiciest Curry Challenge!* When you hear statements like these, you probably smirk, or laugh, or give someone a knowing sideways glance. But as a Sagittarian soul, you love to entertain people, and this can feed into your penchant for exaggeration. And although this style of communication can be very entertaining at times, it can make you seem ungrounded and out of touch with reality when indulged in constantly—and this, in turn, can make you hard to know.

Sagittarian expressions often have bright eyes and big ideals, and this can make it difficult for them to accept the more pedestrian aspects of life. If you have planets in Sagittarius, you may embellish your stories out of an unconscious attempt to make life as dramatic and exciting as you want it to be—or to reimagine yourself as a heroic person who really can pull off incredible feats, every time. As entertaining as these fantastic stories may be, however, they can also be a way of distancing yourself from others and preventing them from seeing the real you. To create trust and reliability, you have to give people an accurate picture of who you are, and what you can and cannot do.

Your Sagittarian love of exaggeration can also get you into trouble sometimes by causing you to over-promise: *I can have that project to you by tomorrow morning! Thanksgiving dinner for twenty-four? No problem!* This tendency is driven by a sincere desire to help others, matched with difficulty making an accurate estimate of how much time, energy, and effort is required to actually meet that deadline. Your soul growth journey involves learning to be grounded in your concept of time, energy, and commitment. You can do this by slowing down, thinking things through, and letting others know what you *can* do—not what you *wish* you could do.

Exercise: Cultivating Self-Acceptance

Sometimes your Sagittarian tendency toward hyperbole comes from a deep-seated fear that you won't be understood or heard unless you exaggerate who you are, or what you've done, or where you've been. When you work to understand and alleviate this fear, it becomes easier for you to release your need to be seen as "exceptional" and accept yourself as you truly are. This visualization exercise can help.

Start by sitting or lying down in a place where you feel safe and comfortable. Take a few deep, centering breaths. When you are ready, visualize a being who represents complete love and acceptance to you. This could be a deity like the Buddha or Quan Yin, or a creature like a dragon. Let your imagination decide.

Imagine that you are looking at yourself through the eyes of this perfectly loving and accepting being. Feel how you are truly understood by the Divine. Feel how you are heard for your perspectives. Feel how this being accepts you exactly as you are; there is *nothing* you can do to make them love you any more or any less.

Practice this visualization for five minutes each day, or whenever you are struggling to be heard or understood.

Exercise: Reframing Expectations

If you have planets in Sagittarius, you may have a hard time distinguishing between what you *want* to give, and what you *can* give—and this leads to over-promising. Luckily, there's an easy way around this!

The next time somebody asks you to do something, simply think out loud, stating what you *want* to do, followed by what you *can* do. For example: "You have no idea how much I'd love to get that project handed in tomorrow morning, but *realistically*, it's going to take me until Friday afternoon."

Reframing expectations in this way can create a connection between your desire and a realistic outcome. It allows you to communicate your sincere wish to solve the other person's problem, while refraining from making promises you can't keep.

Turning Self-Deprecation into Self-Love

As a Saggitarian soul, you are probably an expert at turning your mistakes, slip-ups, and faux pas into hilarious stories that get the whole room laughing. Whether you went to work with your pants on backward or forgot your lines in the high school play, you have no problem making yourself the butt of the joke, especially if it brightens another person's day. Yet these embarrassing episodes that you can spin into comedic gold may be hiding subtle layers of self-judgment and criticism. For all their self-deprecation, Sagittarians can have surprisingly big egos—and humor is often a way of shielding those egos and making sure that nobody sees just how bruised they can be.

Your Sagiattarian energy can make it hard for you to say: "Wow, that was humiliating. I was so embarrassed. I couldn't look anyone in the eye for a week." Instead, you may try to laugh the situation off, while burying the pain or shame associated with it. Although humor is often a sign of resilience, it can also be a way to distract from distressing emotions. Many stand-up comics confess to being anxious or depressed, even as they make entire crowds roar with laughter. This is a familiar dynamic for some Sagittarians.

But your skill for turning embarrassing moments into funny anecdotes is more than just a defense mechanism. It's also a beautiful gift to those around you. It makes space for others to share their own mishaps without fearing judgment, and this can help them move on from embarrassing episodes quickly instead of being defined by them. When you allow yourself to acknowledge your vulnerability, you can embrace your skill for self-deprecation, while engendering self-love and giving others the support they need when they really need it.

Exercise: Practicing Vulnerability

Do you use humor as a way of making people think you're okay—even when you're not? The next time you find yourself turning a painful event into a funny story, ask yourself if you're truly ready to laugh about it, or if it would be more appropriate to ask for support.

Ask your trusted friends if you can tell them the story in a way that *won't* make them laugh. Then tell them the facts of what happened and how you felt about it, without adding or removing details to make it funnier or easier to digest.

Notice what it feels like to let someone in on the truth of your experience— not as an audience member, but as a source of love and support.

Exercise: Ten Years from Now . . .

Everyone makes mistakes sometimes—whether that's turning the wrong way down a one-way street, or forgetting your boss's name. Although these slipups can feel terrible in the moment, they rarely affect us in the long term.

The next time you have an embarrassing moment, imagine yourself ten years in the future. Will you even remember this moment at all? Will anyone else who witnessed it remember it?

Remind yourself that you have probably witnessed other people's most embarrassing moments many times, without even realizing it. If you barely notice someone else's most humiliating moment, what are the chances that other people will pay attention to yours?

Journal Prompts

Consider these questions in the context of what you now know about Sagittarian soul growth. Record your thoughts in your journal so you can return to them as you move forward on the Zodiac wheel.

- Think of a time when someone you respect changed your mind about something. How did that person teach you without making you feel judged or attacked? Which elements of the relationship or interaction made it easy for you to take in that wisdom instead of rejecting it?

- Consider a time when you successfully promised what you *could* do, not what you *wished* you could do. How did it feel to respect your own time and abilities? What circumstances made it easier for you to refrain from over-promising?

- Remember a time when you confided in a friend. How did it feel to tell someone the truth of what you experienced, including all the self-judgment and self-recrimination attached to it? What conditions made it easy for you to confide in your friend instead of trying to entertain?

Chapter 10

Capricorn Soul Growth

♑

Capricorn souls are well-known for being practical, driven, and responsible. They move through the world with a hard-won sense of mastery and accomplishment. Planets in Capricorn are governed by cardinal Earth intentions, which directs them to be productive in the physical world. They often arrive on Earth with a long to-do list, and their strong need to get things done keeps them going long after other star signs have knocked off for the day. Highly competent, well-organized, and clear-headed, they have no problem meeting deadlines, fulfilling promises, and generally following through. They often find themselves in leadership positions, whether that means heading a household or a Fortune 500 company.

Capricorns are often called the "CEOs of the Zodiac." They can feel a lot of pressure to do something important with their lives and rise to the top of their chosen fields or careers. They have a keen sense that time is precious, and often prefer to spend their free time learning, practicing, or honing their skills, rather than kicking back and relaxing. Although their sign is represented by a goat, many Capricorns will tell you that they are *not* here to frolic about. That mountain is for climbing, not for recreation! The ease with which Capricorns can direct their energy can make them seem super-human, which can sometimes arouse jealousy or insecurity in others.

Those with planets in Capricorn are also gifted with patience, which is especially valuable in a world that seeks immediate gratification and instant rewards. They display a level of self-control that others may find elusive. They do their homework every night, knowing they want to get into medical school. They save money carefully, planning ahead for their future comfort and security. But this high degree of self-discipline can sometimes be misunderstood by others, who may find them unforthcoming, reserved, and overly cautious.

Just as mountaineers are willing to scale the highest peaks and endure the storms of nature, Capricorns stay the course to get to their desired outcome, even in the face of extreme obstacles. They stay calm in emergencies, and have the grit and dedication required to navigate difficult situations, whether in business or in their personal lives. But they can also be over-thinkers who hesitate to take action as they weigh the potential downsides of any particular endeavor. They are naturally risk-averse, and sometimes stick to the safer route instead of reaching for the stars.

Because they are such determined achievers, Capricorn expressions can become hyper-focused on the external markers of success and neglect their internal worlds. In the rush to accomplish everything on that to-do list, they may forget to check in with their bodies and hearts on a regular basis. This can sometimes lead to conditions like depression or burnout, as their ambitions outpace their physical energy and sense of meaning. Their soul growth journey involves taking time to listen to that soft inner whisper that reminds them of their soul's true purpose. Their challenge is to hear and respect that whisper, rather than stifling it in the name of their next big achievement.

Competent Capricorns have a lot to offer the people around them. They are natural leaders and loyal friends, and they excel at managing many demands at once and rising to the top of their fields. When this dependable earth sign wakes up to the fact that life isn't one big award ceremony, they can let down their guard, join the ranks of other humans, and discover the innate pleasure of being alive.

The Superhero Trap

Radhi was a strong and self-disciplined Capricorn with a salt-and-pepper beard, a neatly buttoned shirt, and a charming New England accent. When he was a child, his mom had a chronic disease that kept her in bed regularly, while his dad worked long hours at a financial services firm. Radhi had to make his own school lunches and take care of his mother on the weekends, as well as doing his homework, attending violin lessons, studying robotics, and earning Boy Scout badges. Getting things done was a way of life for him. He couldn't conceive of a lazy Sunday; the expression "binge-watching" was not in his vocabulary. Time was meant to be productive, and this attitude had propelled him through college at a top-tier engineering school and launched him on a brilliant career as a computer scientist.

Radhi fell in love with a fellow computer scientist and they adopted a child with special needs. Raising a special-needs child brought out the same superhero tendencies Radhi had honed throughout his life. Even though his child's many health emergencies were a source of stress and anguish to him, he always seemed to rise to the occasion—communicating with doctors and rushing to appointments, while simultaneously pulling off the impossible at work.

Radhi's friends and partner were amazed at his ability to never drop the ball, even when he was under tremendous stress. He seemed able to operate on virtually no sleep, and rarely handed off tasks to others if there was a chance he could do them himself. The same year that he and his partner adopted their daughter, he won a prestigious award for his research in artificial intelligence; the following year, he won an even more prestigious award for his work raising awareness about his daughter's rare disease.

Yet all was not well in this superhero's life. Although Radhi's partner had deep respect and gratitude for his competence as a partner and a parent, he yearned for more vulnerability in their relationship. "Sometimes, I feel like interacting with me is just one more item on your to-do list," he told Radhi one day. "It's one more thing you can excel at—Partner of the Year!—but sometimes I'm not sure that your heart's really in it, or if you're just being great for the sake of being great." He longed to commiserate with Radhi about the stresses of being a parent, but Radhi's refusal to complain meant that he often felt alone in his struggles—or worse, he worried that he was inferior to Radhi.

At work, many of Radhi's team members admired him as a leader, yet felt that he was reluctant to allow them to take on meaningful responsibilities. A few of them even wondered if he hoarded opportunities for himself by denying others the chance to prove themselves. Indeed, Radhi was so invested in his work that he found it hard to "risk" letting anyone else get involved. After all, what if they weren't as competent and responsible as he was? He knew all the things that could go wrong if someone made a mistake, so it always seemed better to remain in control himself.

Like many Capricorns, Radhi relied on his inner strength, strong intentions, and willpower to move through life, and had a hard time letting go and trusting that life would take care of itself. He was a very successful person, and could point to his success as "proof" that his method of living was working. Yet he admitted to me that sometimes his life felt like a never-ending series of tasks to complete and goals to achieve, with no grand meaning to it all. He rarely checked in with his heart or his intuition, and even his body felt to him like a machine he had to maintain rather than a part of himself.

"I feel like a very successful *robot*," he told me. "As if I've been programmed to achieve things, without really understanding why. Sometimes when I'm in the middle of a task, I pop out of it for a second and think: Why am I even chasing these things? And who would I be if I stopped?"

Although Radhi's achievements in life were laudable, he was being called to slow down and tune in to his inner wisdom, and to let the people close to him see him as a real person—not the superhero he wanted to be. His soul growth journey involved learning that self-discipline is a great gift, but so is the ability to soften, go easy on yourself, and let others pick up the slack. As a goal-oriented Capricorn, Radhi tended to project his energy into the future—the next deadline, the next graduation, the next raise, the next promotion—while neglecting the present moment. By sinking into the beauty of the *now*, he could awaken to the fact that there is life outside of constant productivity.

From Public to Personal

Trophies, prizes, certificates, letters after your name—Capricorn planets love putting some energy into acquiring these markers of accomplishment. Even at a young age, you were most likely driven to be successful, no matter how much work it took. Perhaps you grew up idolizing scientists, athletes, or artists who achieved great things. Perhaps your parents modeled success and expected the same of you. You may have carefully and methodically plotted out your path to success, listing all the steps you had to take to achieve your goal, then checking them off one by one.

Capricorn souls pursue whatever they have deemed valuable and important, whether it's an advanced degree, a published book, or a corner office. But with planets in Capricorn, it's important for you to stop and ask yourself what it all *means*. Is that graduate program really the way you want to spend your precious time on Earth? Or is it just a way to get a fancy title before your name? Do you *need* to make more sales than anyone else on your team? Or is success something you seek compulsively? What is the end goal of all this success, and how will you know when you've finally done enough?

At some point on your Capricorn soul growth journey, it will be essential for you to reflect on what you're building, mastering, and achieving to make sure it really matters to *you*—not to your parents, your peers, or the other parents in the PTA. As a Capricorn soul, you are sensitive to the needs and expectations of others. But while this sensitivity can be a wonderful gift, it can also lead you to pursue things just because others want or expect you to, not for your own internal fulfillment. Your challenge is to find your own inherent value and meaning, independent of any external markers of success, and to learn that simply enjoying life can be enough.

Exercise: Cultivating Awe

If you have planets in Capricorn, you may get so focused on your goals and responsibilities that you forget the wonder of simply being alive. Intentionally cultivating awe is a powerful way to remind yourself that life is a miracle, no matter what you achieve.

Every day, spend five minutes looking closely at an element of nature—dewdrops on a leaf, ants marching over a fallen piece of fruit, clouds forming on the horizon.

Give yourself completely to the experience. Don't use this time to think, plan, or problem-solve. Simply absorb the beauty of what you are seeing, and recall the incredible web of life that surrounds you at all times.

Return to this practice whenever you catch yourself getting too caught up in external goals.

Exercise: Connecting with Your Inner Child

As a "CEO of the Zodiac," you run the risk of taking life a little too seriously, and forgetting the carefree child deep inside. This exercise can help you to connect with the part of yourself that loves to skip, jump, and squish your feet in the mud.

Begin by consciously recalling a pleasure you enjoyed as a child—drawing with chalk, lying under a tree and reading an entire book, or taking a bike ride. Allow yourself to experience this memory in as much detail as possible.

Feel the sunlight on your sleeves, the excitement and joy you felt, and the sense of wonder and freedom.

Then give yourself permission to have this experience in your adult life. Grab some art supplies, go play outside, or read every last chapter of that novel as the leaves rustle above your head.

Recognize that your inner child is always with you, even as you bravely navigate the challenges and responsibilities of the adult world. A good CEO always makes room for play!

Releasing Internal Pressure

What's that whistling sound? Is it a boiling teakettle? Or is it your own inner pressure to do it all, be the best, and keep moving forward? When the going gets tough, your Capricorn energy often responds by pushing harder—putting in more hours, increasing your effort, and even self-flagellating—when what you really need to do is to take a step back and learn to trust. Like the rugged mountain goat, you may deal with internal tension by commanding yourself to "just be stronger." But all too often, this creates anxiety, stress, and sleepless nights. When you push too hard, you can wear out your body *and* your mind—and that doesn't do anyone any good.

With planets in Capricorn, you are very strong and capable of taking on the world—but sometimes moving forward means falling back. Sometimes, when you hear that internal voice telling you to be responsible, keep it all together, and never show weakness, you need to decline respectfully. After all, you can't keep it all together if you're lying awake all night thinking about how to deliver that project on time, or taking on so many responsibilities that you collapse. Learning to encourage and support yourself, rather than relentlessly driving yourself, can be immensely valuable.

A key component of your soul growth is to allow yourself not to take life so seriously and to learn to trust that everything that is important will get done. You do not have to carry the weight of the world for everyone, or assume that you are the only one qualified to handle it all. In fact, you may start to feel your energy shift and lighten the more you delegate and allow others to take on their fair share. You may tend to be overly controlling, either because you do not trust others to do things the right way, or because you feel so invested in the outcome of a project that you don't want to take any chances. But when you learn to fall back and trust in the gifts of others, you experience the joy that comes from true collaboration and achieve even greater success.

Exercise: Softening Your Self-Talk

You may unconsciously crank up the pressure by letting your internal voice run wild with suggestions, directions, and instructions that may masquerade as helpful encouragement: *Just one more hour of work. I know you can do it!*

Try practicing a softer form of self-talk using phrases like these:

- ◆ Do I need to rest?

- ◆ I've done enough today.

- ◆ It's time to relax; _____ has got this under control.

By consciously inserting these thoughts into your mind, you can soften into life, receiving what you want instead of pushing for it.

Exercise: Trusting Others

Control-freak Capricorn energy can have a hard time relying on others. You can counter this tendency and learn to build your trust in others by making small requests of them on a regular basis.

For example, ask your neighbor to collect your mail while you're on vacation, or ask your daughter to feed the dog. Eventually, you can build up to bigger acts of trust, like collaborating on a project at work.

Notice how it feels to let others take care of tasks you would normally do yourself. What would it be like if you could *always* assume that other people were as diligent as you are?

Embracing Your Humanity

It's a bird! It's a plane! It's a Capricorn! Yes, the man of steel and Capricorns have a lot in common. Both have a clever way of hiding their humanity and vulnerabilities from the world. Just as Superman can appear to take on the world and handle all problems, Capricorn souls are equipped with the ability to take care of anything and everything. But let's be real. Even Superman has his weaknesses and vulnerabilities. So what's your kryptonite?

Capricorn energy can project so much competence that you may leave others feeling awed—or insecure. When you promise to do something, you do it—even if it means getting up at four in the morning, driving through snow, and working yourself into a state of exhaustion. This quality of ultra-responsibility can make you a valuable friend and partner. But sometimes those around you may find themselves wishing that *just this once* you'd let your hair down, eat a pint of ice cream, and veg out on the couch while the deadline rolls past. Being hitched to such a self-disciplined person can make others feel as if they're constantly being left in the dust.

Your Capricorn soul can grow when you learn to embrace your own humanity and give up your superhero image. You may be more comfortable hiding any evidence that you, too, need to eat, sleep, and unwind. But showing your softer side can give others a chance to feel that you're one of them, not a figure on a pedestal high above them. When you *only* project an unshakeable image, you prevent others from truly knowing you. But when you relax into your own blunders, mistakes, and moments of exhaustion, you allow people to see your real self, and this builds trust and relatability.

Exercise: Plop Time

Do you spend every waking moment moving from one task to the next? Intentionally building some "plop time" into your day can help you remember that life isn't all about work. And this can help you connect with your friends or family.

Every evening, set aside thirty minutes in which you engage in a low-key, unstructured activity that is *not* goal-oriented or "productive." Play video games with your roommates, or chat on the porch with your neighbors.

Notice how the simple act of kicking back and unwinding with the people around you puts you in touch with the inherent pleasure of being human, whether or not you're ascending to great heights.

Exercise: Showing Your Soft Spot

Do you feel the need to solve others' problems for them, whether or not you really know how? Do you feel pressured to project knowledge that you don't always have rather than admitting uncertainty?

The next time someone comes to you with a problem, let them see you struggle with it instead of confidently laying out a plan. For example, say: "Wow, that's really tough. I wish I knew the right thing to do, but I don't."

Try joining your friends and loved ones in their challenges, instead of setting yourself apart as the person who always knows what to do.

Journal Prompts

Consider these questions in the context of what you now know about Capricorn soul growth. Record your thoughts in your journal so you can return to them as you move forward on the Zodiac wheel.

- Consider a time when you felt happy just to be alive—perhaps while walking in nature, or spending time with a child. How did it feel to be happy even though you weren't accomplishing anything "important"? What conditions made it possible for you to be happy in that moment?

- Recall a time when you were able to soften into life instead of pushing yourself harder to achieve. What was it like to allow life to take care of you instead of feeling that you had to take care of life?

◆ Think of a time when you let your guard down—answered the door in your slippers, admitted you weren't sure, or called in sick. How did it feel to put down the burden of always being "on"? Did everything fall apart for the people around you, or did they manage?

Chapter 11

Aquarius Soul Growth

Aquarius, the eleventh sign of the Zodiac, is a fixed air sign whose energies engender strong minds and keen intellects. Because this sign is represented by a water bearer, people often mistakenly think of it as a water sign, but this figure actually represents the pouring of consciousness out of a container to benefit the collective in some way. Planets in Aquarius are filled with independence, curiosity, and a creative spark. They bring a new frequency to the spaces and places through which they move, and often have the capacity to see the big picture or bring a different perspective to mundane circumstances.

Although Aquarian expressions often refuse to get involved in activities that don't resonate with them, once they do find a cause that inspires them, they become loyal to it for the long term. They may volunteer at the same organization for decades, fundraising many thousands of dollars. They become deeply involved with social movements or political parties, sometimes giving their lives to causes they believe in. But if you try to tell them what to do or how to do it, they'll be gone in a flash.

People with planets in Aquarius are always brimming with ideas and opinions, and can be great conversationalists. They may enjoy engaging in satisfying debates; their love for playing devil's advocate can be so strong that it's hard to tell what they really stand for, and when they are just making an argument for argument's sake. They may enjoy stirring the pot with the intention of getting people to think, discuss, and understand an issue from multiple viewpoints. If others are offended, even better—because then they can talk about why that opinion may be limited (Ha!).

This air sign has intellect to spare, and many Aquarians burn off that excess mental energy by considering issues from many sides and engaging in verbal sparring matches with anyone who's willing to argue. Just don't try to engage them in small talk, because they'll quickly get bored and walk away.

Aquarians are good at thinking systematically, and are drawn to careers in technology, data, science, and engineering. But they also care deeply about the public good, and often become teachers, social workers, counselors, and humanitarian workers. Although they are skilled at closing off their own emotions, they openly express their care for others through acts of service. They may not gush all over you or spill their hearts out, but they *will* fix your alternator and show you how to update your phone.

Aquarian expressions can be contrarian, and rebel against the status quo. They can get prickly when others place expectations on them, especially when it comes to emotional availability. They also have a not-so-subtle need to break free from anything that is too restraining, especially any extended hugs. At the same time, many may feel an unconscious need to fit in, to belong, or to be part of a larger group. They are energetically designed to connect with a collective. However, for them, the group dynamic serves as a vehicle for acquiring deeper self-knowledge, not as a way of ditching their individuality. Their soul growth unfolds through a journey of collective connections *and* independent enlightenment.

Intellectual Aquarians are anything but airheads—and when they learn to hold their watery parts with skill and confidence, they can be loyal friends and committed partners. Whether they're in a lone wolf phase or running with a pack, Aquarian souls always give the best of themselves to causes they believe in, making the world a better place for all.

Will's Tribe

Will was a magnetic Aquarian who knew from a young age that his path through life would not always be easy. The child of troubled parents, he grew up bouncing from foster home to foster home in a gritty part of Chicago. It was hard for him to develop a sense of belonging with either his foster parents or his fellow foster children, because he never knew when he would be moved again and lose those relationships forever.

This sense of uncertainty made it hard for Will to "find his tribe." He wasn't a joiner, and wasn't about to change any aspect of himself to fit in with kids at school. This made it difficult for him to make friends, but it also protected him. When gang members tried to recruit him, he declined to join them, a decision that probably saved him a lot of heartache, and may even have saved his life.

Will always felt that he was on the outside looking in. He learned to observe the social dynamics of his foster homes, and of his junior and senior high schools.

Over the years, he became quite adept at reading people. He could tell a lot about others from their body language, their posture, the tilt of their head, and their facial expressions. By the time he was a teenager, he had also realized that he was quite a bit more intelligent than most of his peers, and even some of the adults in his life. And he sometimes took pleasure in provoking others by leading them into debates in which he played devil's advocate to their deeply held beliefs.

Will probably could have spent his whole life as an outsider. But, when he was twenty, he got a job as a youth counselor at the local community center. Suddenly, after all this time, he had found his tribe. Every Friday, he played basketball with the other counselors and with their wise and big-hearted boss and mentor. As they shot hoops, they debriefed after their full days of work running summer programs for neighborhood kids. When one of the counselors was evicted from his home, the others pulled together to find him a place to stay and helped him come up with a rental deposit.

"I'd never experienced that kind of love, loyalty, and belonging in my whole life," Will told me, tearing up as he recalled those golden years.

Twenty years later, Will became the director of the youth program, overseeing a team of counselors who reminded him a lot of his old tribe. He'd gone back to school for a master's degree in social work, and he took pride in the organization he worked for, which did so much to help foster kids. He maintained the Friday night basketball tradition, and his team of counselors looked up to him. But his old devil's-advocate tendencies sometimes got him in trouble, because he loved to needle the next generation about their "millennial" values and political views.

After having one serious relationship in his thirties, Will had settled into bachelorhood and sworn off dating forever. Although he couldn't admit it to himself, his ex-girlfriend had been the love of his life, but when she repeatedly tried to push through his emotional avoidance, he had denied there was a problem. She had also complained that Will was "hot and cold," paying lots of attention to her on some days, only to disconnect abruptly and retreat into himself for no apparent reason. Meanwhile, Will couldn't understand how she could have expected him to be so consistent. Didn't everyone need to unplug sometimes?

Like many Aquarians, Will longed to be part of something greater than himself, but he also wanted to do his own thing, on his own terms. And he preferred to leave the past in the past, even when his childhood wounds resurfaced. In fact, he never even told his ex-girlfriend about his childhood experiences in foster care, and they were together for six years!

"I didn't want her pity, or anyone else's," he told me. "I'm living the life I want to live. Why should I bring up things that happened thirty years ago?" He also associated emotional vulnerability with self-indulgence. "I think those millennials are way off-base, always talking about their trauma and their therapy. Just get on with life! Instead of crying about your past, go out and make the future brighter for someone else."

There's no doubt that Will was making a difference in the lives of the youths he mentored. Far from navel-gazing, he was taking positive action in the world. But to grow to his full potential, he had to learn to connect authentically with others instead of holding them at arm's length or treating them as debate partners. He needed to open himself up in order to find his tribe once more.

Focusing on Heartfelt Connections

If you have planets in Aquarius, you know you can find a way to turn *anything* into a debate. Sure, we should save the whales—but have you considered the fact that whales emit carbon dioxide? And just think of how many poor, helpless krill they eat every year! Yup, there's nothing your Aquarian soul loves more than watching people get vexed, flustered, or even downright upset when you poke holes in commonly held truths. Whether you're playing devil's advocate in an argument between friends or acting contrarily just for the fun of it, you probably enjoy a good debate the way other signs enjoy going for a satisfying run.

Luckily for you—or not?—social media has made it possible to exchange thoughts, opinions, and ideologies with a wide range of people, all day long. Many Aquarian souls are avid internet users, making valuable contributions to the online communities they frequent, and scoring important points for the causes they care about. But if this is the case for you, you must be careful not to turn into a troll who engages with others just to provoke them. Over time, this can alienate not just strangers on the internet but your friends and family as well, who may feel that you are flaunting your intellect or even using it to bully others.

Although it can be hard to admit, the desire to provoke can also be a defense mechanism that keeps your conversations from going to an uncomfortably tender or emotional place. You can experience tremendous soul growth when you bring more intentionality to how you share your thoughts. You need to ask yourself: Am I saying this to deepen my connection with this person—or to push them away?

Exercise: The Hammer and the Nail

When you're holding a hammer, everything looks like a nail—and if you're an Aquarian soul with a keen intellect, everything may appear to call for an intellectual approach, even when an emotional response may be more appropriate.

The next time you find yourself in conversation with those close to you, ask yourself what they are looking for. Are they trying to engage you in an intellectual debate? Or are they trying to connect emotionally? If you're not sure, it's okay to ask. For example: "Do you want my intellectual analysis, or are you looking for comfort right now?"

Simply asking whether or not an intellectual response is appropriate can help you shift out of the habit of using that hammer exclusively, and teach you to pick up other tools.

Exercise: "First, understand."

If you enjoy playing devil's advocate, you may not realize how this comes across to those looking to you for emotional support. For example, a child who was bullied at school may feel even more rejected if you insist on "seeing the other side" before tending to their pain.

The next time you find yourself automatically playing devil's advocate, pause and mentally say the words: "First, understand." Then ask the other person: "Can you explain what you're going through and why you feel the way you do?"

Notice if the other person is coming to you for emotional support, or just wants an intellectual spin on the situation.

Once you feel that you truly understand the situation, you can either go ahead and play devil's advocate—if it still feels appropriate—or you can switch to a different mode.

Embracing Emotional Truths

Those with planets in Aquarius often focus on the intellectual components of a topic or issue. After all, who needs to talk about feelings when you can discuss all the new gadgets you've read about in *WIRED* magazine, or debate the latest political news, or plan your next computer upgrade? You may struggle to stay engaged in emotional exchanges as you attempt to deflect or distract, or bring them to a close prematurely. Over time, this reluctance to engage emotionally can wear out your friends and partners, and sometimes even lead them to end the relationship.

Aquarian souls may find it hard to connect to the emotional persectives of others. After all, their brains are always busily working on problems which may be taking place in an entirely different—and safer—dimension. And if the emotions are uncomfortable, all the more reason to stay on that safe, intellectual plane. But over time, this emotional avoidance becomes a form of debt that can become harder and harder for the Aquarian soul to pay back.

You can grow by acknowledging that dodging emotional connection is just as harmful as dodging other forms of reciprocity in relationships. When you form an intention to engage with others, however, you can become a deeply supportive partner and friend, while meeting emotional needs you didn't even realize you had. Although at first you may claim to feel bored or restless when faced with emotional demands, these feelings are often covering up a deep uncertainty. As you learn to tune in to your watery nature, this uncertainty dissolves, paving the way to deep and sustaining connections.

Exercise: Recognizing Exit Strategies

If you have planets in Aquarius, you may not even realize when you're being emotionally avoidant. Learning to recognize your emotional "exit strategies" is the first step to gently releasing them.

Over the next week, pay attention to what you do when someone asks you to engage emotionally. Do you find an urgent task that needs attention? Do you promise to talk about it later? Do you express frustration that the other person has an emotional need at all?

Make a list of these strategies, and practice recognizing when you feel tempted to use them.

Over time, the simple process of noticing when you want to avoid emotions will help you make different choices.

Exercise: Initiating Emotional Encounters

Aquarian expressions tend to feel ambushed by other people's emotional needs. To get around this, make a practice of consciously initiating emotional encounters yourself.

Once a week, make a point of asking your friends or partner to connect with you emotionally. For example, ask them how they feel about a recent event, or share how you felt about something that happened to you.

By "getting out ahead" of emotional encounters, you can begin to stop seeing them as threats, and more as gestures you're *choosing* to make.

Expanding Beyond Your Tribe

Aquarian souls can be particular about joining in, but once they find their tribe, they enjoy a sense of belonging that fills their hearts and gives them a sense of pride. When they go to summer camp, they either return year after year, proclaiming their lifelong loyalty to the Best Cabin Ever, or spend the summer completely alone, rejecting all attempts to draw them into the group and vowing never to return. This fickle air sign may seek out collective vibes on a regular basis, or prefer to be left alone in a cabin in the woods for years at a time—there's really no way to predict which way the coin will fall.

If you have planets in Aquarius, you may equate fitting in with intellectual compatibility. Do these people get me? Or do I need to dumb myself down for them to accept me? You would probably rather eat lunch alone in the library than sit with a herd of others with whom you don't feel compatible. On the other hand, when you find your tribe—whether that's a chess club, a rugby team, or an astronomy society—you light up like a firecracker, bringing the full sparkle of your mind and personality to bear on the situation at hand.

You may also experience long stretches of time when you don't have a tribe, and periods of life when you do—and both of these conditions are just fine. Be patient; the right people will come along, and you will be glad you waited instead of joining up with an incompatible group. You can also grow by inviting a wider range of social connections into your life. Sure, your coworkers may not be your soul mates, but would it kill you to go to that baby shower? Making space for casual acquaintances and people who fall outside your intellectual wheelhouse can make your life richer and more fun. Although you may be happiest in your tribe, you might be surprised by how nice it can be to make alliances with other tribes as well.

Exercise: "Just Like Me . . . "

Are you in the habit of instantly filtering people into categories: boring/interesting, my tribe/not my tribe, and so on? In this exercise, I invite you to expand your concept of who "your" people are.

The next time you meet someone new, take a moment to remind yourself of your common humanity. You can do this by repeating the following phrases:

- "Just like me, this person needs comfort when they are in distress."

- "Just like me, this person needs rest when they are exhausted."

- "Just like me, this person needs care when they are sick."

Try coming up with your own variations on these phrases. By repeating them to yourself when you meet new people, you can connect with your shared humanity, instead of sorting people into categories.

Exercise: Calling in Your Tribe

If it's been a while since you've had a tribe of friends or collaborators with whom you really felt compatible, it's natural to start feeling lonely. This exercise can remind you that your people *are* out there, and help pave the way energetically for you to find them.

Begin by sitting in a comfortable position. Take a few deep breaths to center and ground yourself. Then bring your mind to an awareness that, just as you have found your tribe in the past, you will soon find meaningful friends once more.

Feel the presence of these new friends just at the edge of your awareness. Then bring to mind all the other people in the world who are likewise looking for connection.

Send a gentle wish to the Universe that all of these people will find their tribes, just as you want to find yours.

Journal Prompts

Consider these questions in the context of what you now know about Aquarian soul growth. Record your thoughts in your journal so you can return to them as you near the end of your journey around the Zodiac wheel.

- Recall a time when you had an emotional conversation with another person. What made it easy for you to open up emotionally? What made it possible for you to stay in that space instead of pushing things into debate mode?

- Think of a time when you assented to a friend's or partner's emotional needs, instead of trying to bypass them. What made it easy for you to be there for them? How did it feel to be able to give them what they needed?

- Consider a time when you became friends with someone you didn't connect with at first. What was it like to discover a side of that person that you truly enjoyed? How would your life be different if you'd never made that connection?

Chapter 12

Pisces Soul Growth

Pisces is the twelfth and final sign of the Zodiac. This mutable water sign is represented by two fish swimming in opposite directions, and Pisces is associated with the ocean depths. Thus planets in Pisces can sometimes struggle to adjust to life on dry land. If they had their way, many of them would spend their whole lives navigating the watery dimensions of their inner worlds, paying little attention to the nuts and bolts of everyday life. Piscean energies can sometimes feel overly stimulated by the "real world," with its deadlines, obligations, and sensory overload, and must take special care to recharge their batteries after school or work.

Piscean souls are gifted with wonderful imaginations and arrive on Earth with a deep connection to their intuition. They seek out creative outlets like dance, music, and the visual arts that encourage them to express their inner worlds. They are drawn to careers in filmmaking, choreography, art therapy, or spiritual services, in which they can develop their creative and empathic strengths. When Pisceans find kindred spirits with whom to collaborate, their creative energy can go to a whole new level. But when they are placed on a team or group project with more rational, logical expressions, they can struggle to integrate their different approaches.

Planets in Pisces are compassionate by nature, and bring a spirit of loving kindness to the collective energy field. If you've ever received a random act of kindness from a stranger, whether that's a much-needed compliment or a cup of coffee on the house, there's a good chance your benefactor was a Pisces. They are always attuned to the needs of those around them, and they are natural givers. In fact, in some cases, this trait can be so strong that it leads to excessive self-sacrifice and over-commitment. Piscean souls must take care to remain aware of whether they are staying in a job or relationship because it's really the best thing for them, or if they're only staying because other people "need" them.

Planets in Pisces represent the energy of surrender, dissolution, completion, and transcendence. Many Pisces souls enjoy the feeling of surrender so much that they seek it out wherever they can find it, whether that's in trance states or meditation, or by working with plant medicines or other spiritual practices. In some cases, however, their love of transcendence can turn into escapism, as the spiritual practice becomes a way of avoiding the commitments, responsibilities, and monotony of the everyday world.

The Piscean experience is often centered on figuring out where to go—in their lives, in their careers, or just when doing the grocery shopping. Unlike others who come to Earth knowing exactly what they came here to do, Pisces placements tend to take a more meandering route, swimming through careers and relationships with no fixed destination. This can be a source of confusion or frustration to many of them, so it's important they remember that they are being guided by a larger energy stream than their conscious minds recognize. At a soul level, they are here to keep trusting where the energy is pulling them without becoming overly fixated on what is right, wrong, good, or bad. They are here for all of it, and this sets them apart from others' experiences.

Piscean souls are scaly, slippery, and ever-elusive. They only come to the surface for so long before darting back into the depths. When these empathic beings learn to balance their intuitive and watery natures with the demands of the physical world, however, they can be a source of inspiration to everyone around them, experiencing tremendous freedom while forging the deep relationships that come from commitment.

Fantasy Film

Cara was a young social media influencer known for her vegan cooking tips. She spent many hours a day photographing herself in the kitchen of her shared apartment, whipping up dairy-free mac and cheese, or visiting the many plant-based cafes and vegan boutiques in her hip urban neighborhood. She even had a cruelty-free hair and makeup regimen that she documented religiously on her smartphone. As far as her followers knew, she was a full-time social media star. In reality, she had a distinctly unglamorous day job as a home healthcare aide.

As a dreamy and evanescent Pisces, Cara had always taken refuge in her imagination. She'd spent most of elementary school with her head in the clouds, coming down to Earth only when the teacher called on her. She loved to draw, and often drew pages and pages of fantasies, most of them revolving around a princess in a turreted castle surrounded by rose gardens. As a teenager, she switched from drawing to writing, and spent every evening creating future installments of her favorite fantasy fiction series and posting them online.

Cara's imagination was a reliable escape in a life that was often disappointing. She never imagined she'd be stuck in a low-paying job well into her twenties, but her social media channel allowed her to live a more fulfilling "second life" in which every day was sunny, and she always woke up looking beautiful. In fact, she got so much pleasure out of tending her online identity that she often slipped out of *real* social events early to get home and prepare posts. Real friends knew that she was struggling to pay her rent, but her online followers imagined that she was well-off—and that made her feel great.

Cara had a gift for seeing the best in people, and tended to make friends in unlikely places. She became close to several of the elderly people she served in her day job, and had good relationships with her two roommates. But when it came to romantic relationships, her imagination sometimes clouded her judgment. When she first came to me, she'd recently broken up with a film producer who was nearly ten years older than she was. He had practically moved in with her just weeks after they met, much to her roommates' consternation.

"They both tried to tell me there was something off about him," Cara admitted, "but I was so swept up in this fantasy of who he was that I couldn't listen."

The man told Cara he was about to start work on a very exciting film, and was taking a few weeks off before the project started. He stayed home while she went to work and, when she came home, he was often sleeping. "I thought he was just taking a nap after working on his film script and going to the gym," Cara said. "He seemed like such a hard worker, even when he was taking time off—and I never liked telling him 'no.'"

But when her roommates found a cache of empty liquor bottles under the kitchen sink, Cara realized that the man was an alcoholic. The "exciting film" he was supposed to be working on never materialized, and when one of her roommates came home early one day to find him lying in the living room drunk, Cara agreed to tell him to move out right away.

Like many Pisceans, Cara's fantasies were so powerful that she sometimes confused them with reality. In order to reach her soul's potential in this lifetime, she needed to expand her willingness to "touch down" in the real world, even as she gave herself the freedom to fly in her imagination. By tapping into her inner strength, she could learn to approach relationships from a position of strength, and find ways to make her life in the physical world as satisfying and meaningful as the life she lived in her dreams.

Balancing Surrender with Intention

The Piscean capacity for surrender is a beautiful gift. Unlike other signs that struggle to let go of their thinking, planning minds, Piscean souls have a wonderful ability to just slip away into the realms of the imagination. Far from wasting their lives in pointless battles, they can easily let go of the things that aren't that important to them. Whether during arguments with romantic partners or sticky situations at work, they are likely to shrug their shoulders and say: "Sure, have it your way," paving the way to peace rather than duking things out to the bitter end.

But there's a fine line between being a peacemaker and being a pushover. If you have planets in Pisces, you must be careful not to cross it. In some cases, your surrender instinct can turn into defeatism, and you may find it easier just to give up rather than leaning into a hard conversation or a tough situation. You may find yourself surrendering in situations where it would be healthier to stand up for yourself. A key aspect of your soul growth will be learning to tap into your inner strength when you find yourself in conflict with others. Are you *truly* happy with letting others have their way? Or are you just in the habit of saying "yes"?

When you surrender too easily or too often, you can find that your course in life is set by your friends, partner, or coworkers, rather than by your intention. *Sure, I can transfer to the Kansas office. Okay, I'll adopt your cat. You want your mom to move in with us? No problem.* When this happens, you can end up living a life that doesn't exactly feel like *yours*, and is defined by the wants and needs of those around you. You can grow by taking the time to define your own vision for your life intentionally, even as you graciously sway with the desires of others.

Exercise: Buying Time

If you're a Piscean soul who's in the habit of giving in to avoid conflict, it can feel very daunting to start standing up for your needs and preferences. As a first step, you can establish a habit of simply buying time rather than saying "yes" right away.

The next time a friend, partner, boss, or coworker pushes you to agree to something, simply say: "I need a few minutes to process this. Let me get back to you shortly."

Then go for a short walk or sit in a room where you can lean into your feelings and think your thoughts without any pressure to give a response. Notice if you genuinely want to surrender to the other person's will, or if your "yes" was just a knee-jerk reaction.

By establishing a habit of buying time, you can pave the way to giving authentic responses, rather than immediately surrendering.

Exercise: Knowing What's Yours

Some planets in Pisces surrender too easily because they are highly empathic, and find it too uncomfortable to feel other people's disappointment or frustration if they don't get what they want. This exercise invites you to draw a clear line around the emotions that are yours, and those that belong to others.

The next time you feel sensitive to others' disappointment or frustration, visualize a gentle container surrounding them—an orb of light, a beautiful basket, or anything else you choose. Know that their difficult emotions are safely held within this container—there is no need for you to hold them on their behalf.

Return to this exercise any time you feel tempted to surrender for the sole purpose of managing someone else's emotions.

Boosting Your Staying Power

If you've ever invited a Pisces to a party, you know they're masters of the "Irish exit"—that cute but maddening practice of slipping out the door without saying goodbye. And if you have Pisces placements yourself, you also know that you sometimes just need to get out and disappear—for reasons you don't always understand. Because of your intuitive and empathic soul, you can find that your social batteries are easily drained, sometimes with little warning. In other cases, however, you may just be behaving like the slippery fish you are. And that elusiveness can be hard for friends, partners, and coworkers to handle over the long term.

Piscean energy, like the ocean, wants to ebb and flow without restraint. But that doesn't give you a free pass to just wander out halfway through an online meeting, or mentally check out when you're on a hike with friends. Real life calls you to stay present even when you're bored or tired or when the "fun part" is over. You may find yourself challenged to find ways to cultivate your need for freedom and openness without turning into a total flake. After all, your freedom often depends on other people picking up the slack, staying until closing time, and pushing through the tedious parts of a job.

But when you boost your naturally slippery nature with persistence and staying power, you can discover the riches that arise from seeing things through. After all, if you always leave the party early, you never get to participate in the intimate discussions that only happen when the last few guests are left cleaning up. Your surreptitious exit may relieve your internal pressure for a moment, but it robs you of deep social bonds in the long term. By developing your tolerance for seeing things through, you can unlock opportunities that only come to those who stay the course.

Exercise: Raising Your Distress Tolerance

The next time you feel tempted to duck out on a social situation or work meeting, challenge yourself to stay for an additional fifteen minutes.

What happens when you allow those feelings of urgency to simply exist, rather than acting on them right away? Does the urgency build? Or do you get a second wind that carries you through the rest of the gathering?

When you build your tolerance for uncomfortable feelings, you soon learn that they are suggestions for action, not commands, and this can boost your ability to stay the course.

Exercise: More Carrots!

If you have a hard time making it to the end of a social event or work commitment, you can motivate yourself by placing some "carrots" near the finish line.

For example, make plans with a coworker to go out for cupcakes when the meeting is over, or arrange to sing "Happy Birthday" to your friend at the very *end* of the night. You can't leave before singing, can you?

By placing some "carrots" at the end of events, instead of gobbling them up at the beginning, you can give yourself a wonderful reason to stick around.

From Fantasy to Reality

Piscean souls are gifted with rich imaginations. They are dreamers, and liars, and magic-bean buyers (thank you, Shel Silverstein). If this is your sign, your capacity for fantasy is a wonderful thing, especially when it comes to creating works of art. But when it comes to evaluating potential friends and life partners, that same gift can make it difficult for you to see people for who they really are. You always want to see the best in people, and can weave elaborate tales about their heroic qualities, while losing sight of the person right in front of you. When the fantasy fades and that person's true colors start to come into focus, you can be surprised at the size of the gap between the perfection you imagined and the reality you face.

If you've ever found yourself gushing about the *perfect* new person you started dating, chances are you have Pisces placements. For you, the romantic ride can be so intense and exhilarating that it can take you weeks or even months to come down from cloud nine and take a close look at the human being you're actually crushing on. Your desire to transcend the mundane aspects of the real world can cause you to develop a kind of willful blindness that leads you to ignore conventional explanations in favor of fantastical stories. *Is he* really *preternaturally attuned to animals, or did he just have a dog biscuit in his pocket that one time?*

And your tendency to idealize probably isn't limited to other people. You can also indulge in some heavy-duty fantasizing about yourself. Given a set of filters and a few minutes of photo editing, you can transform your humdrum life into a glamorous spectacle worthy of the silver screen. Although there's nothing wrong with mentally reframing your everyday activities to fit a positive narrative, you risk getting so caught up in this process that you lose track of your actual life, and forget where you really are relative to where you imagine yourself to be. By learning to tune in to the facts of a situation, you can gain a greater acceptance of yourself and others as they really are—no fantasy required.

Exercise: Social Media Fast

If you are the kind of Pisces who loves to see and be seen on social media, try taking a one-week fast from your platform of choice.

What happens when you stop arranging your life for the camera? Do you feel lost and empty? Or do you find it easier to be present? How do you spend your time differently when the only person in the audience is *you*?

Exercise: Seeing the Negative

Although it may sound strange at first, some Pisces expressions can benefit from learning to see the *negative* in others, especially when they are in the throes of idealization.

The next time you find yourself becoming infatuated with others, take a few minutes to list their flaws and incompatibilities, no matter how minor. For example, maybe your new paramour drinks coffee, while you are a tea snob. Or maybe a friend seems a little reluctant to talk about their emotions.

The point here isn't to find reasons to dislike or reject people, but merely to acknowledge the dimensions of relationships that may be challenging down the road, instead of fantasizing about pure perfection.

Journal Prompts

Consider these questions in the context of what you now know about Piscean soul growth. Record your thoughts in your journal so you can return to them as you complete your journey around the Zodiac wheel.

- Remember a time when you advocated for yourself instead of surrendering. How did it feel to push for what you needed? Which elements of the situation made it possible for you to do this instead of immediately backing down?

- Consider a time when someone was there for you until the very end—like a sibling who stayed by your side until you'd submitted those college applications, or a partner who took you to every last appointment after you broke your leg. How did it feel to have a person give you that kind of constancy? What would it be like for you to offer that kind of commitment to someone else?

◆ Recall a time when you hung out with an old friend—someone you know deeply. What did it feel like to spend time with someone whose flaws you already knew? What did it feel like to spend time with someone who was already familiar with the parts of *you* that aren't perfect?

Conclusion

Soul Growth Continues On

Your soul growth opportunities will continue to come alive through your astrological signature with your intentional awareness. Caterpillars come into the world with the potential to become butterflies; inconspicuous brown seeds come into being with the potential to become complex and colorful flowers. And you come to your journey on Earth brimming with potential as well. Some aspects of your energies may show themselves early on—like Leo's panache or Capricorn's practicality—while other aspects may need careful tending to reveal themselves in full. Just as a plain, small flower seed gives few hints as to the marvel waiting to emerge, your soul's potential isn't always obvious. I hope that this book has given you the clues you need to uncover your own capacity for growth, based on your unique astrological incarnation and self-reflection.

Whether you came to Earth with planets in Aries, Pisces, or any number of other astrological combinations, know that you have all the tools you need to manifest the highest expression of your particular blend of energies. Although at times it may seem like your energy is comfortable in certain expressions—right down to those tiny quirks and preferences that are so representative of your planetary placements—you also have a choice about how to embody those traits in your day-to-day life. Will you use your Aquarian intellect to dominate others, or to serve the collective at a higher level? Will you let your Scorpio skepticism distance you from others, or serve as a catalyst for greater trust? By engaging fully with the aspects of your chart that challenge you, you can transform those challenges into brilliant opportunities for growth.

True soul growth doesn't mean rejecting uncomfortable traits, but rather embracing them and channeling them for the highest good. Your soul *wants* to learn and grow—otherwise, you wouldn't have chosen to come here. Sure, everyone's journey will look different, but we're all searching for meaning, purpose, and a deep sense of belonging. Some paths may be quiet and peaceful, while others may involve a white-knuckle ride. But at the end of the day, we're all just stardust, endlessly cycling between the Earth and the cosmos. Journey after journey, life after life, we are all learning how to love, to forgive, and to celebrate the mysteries of existence.

With each lifetime your soul spends on Earth, you have a new chance to explore, to discover, and to grow. How can you show up in relationships? How can you fulfill your dreams? What is it like to take risks? What is it like to play things a little safer? What happens if you depend more on others—or find more strength and independence within yourself? What happens if you show up on Earth with these particular tools—or with a different set entirely? Birth after birth, your soul gets to experience life from a multitide of different angles, always evolving to be kinder, wiser, and more compassionate.

No matter what you are going through in this lifetime, I wish you love, courage, and laughter as you walk, skip, or run along your path. Know that every challenge you experience is just as sacred as your joys and successes. Remember that you are learning and growing, each and every day. The forces of the Universe are always there to support your process of unfolding, just as the rain and sun support the seed's transition into a flower. Your soul was born with infinite potential, and continues to have infinite potential until the day you leave the Earth again. May you shine brightly while you endlessly transform.

Acknowledgments

We've all heard that "it takes a village" to raise a child, but I'm pretty sure the same can be said for authors as they move through the full creative process. I am grateful to the village known as the Hierophant Publishing team for their diligence, professionalism, and suggestions that have improved this book from one raw idea to a final, more polished version.

Randy Davila, thank you once again for your leadership, wisdom, and guidance on crafting a new-to-us astrology book. I appreciate your patience with my wild schedule, and your ongoing commitment to excellence in each project.

A highlight of my work since 2021 has been meeting and connecting with many of you in person at retreats, events, and classes. Thank you for showing up to introduce yourselves and share more of who you are with me. We need these in-person connections more than ever during the digital age, and I never take them for granted. Thank you for making time in your busy lives for more astrology!

On a more personal note, I am grateful beyond words to have a global tribe of sisters who offer support, laughter, perspective, and friendship during the highs and lows of life. We need other people who "get us" with loving kindness, especially when life is crazy and I am being pulled in multiple directions. Thank you to my dear girlfriends Natali, Rehana, Sass, Mari, Ava, Tracy, and Trisha for being exactly who you are in this world. I deeply appreciate your wisdom, laughter, and brilliance. My cup runneth over.

We don't have forever on this planet, of course, so it's important to me to make ongoing memories with the people I have known the longest, aka my family. We all live in different corners of the United States (literally—Seattle, Los Angeles, Philadelphia, and Florida), so the opportunities that we can gather in person and experience adventures together are precious and valuable to me. I am grateful that astrology has offered us even more chances to do so, from retreats to dinners; cruises to weddings; and all of the family holidays in the Florida sunshine. Cheers to more chances to gather and remind Oliver that it's his turn to do the dishes.

And definitely not to be forgotten is the seeker who feels called to their astrology chart (you!). I hope this ancient language is reconnecting you with more of who you are here to be in the world right now. It takes great courage, trust, and faith to open up to more of yourself, and yet that is one of the innate promises of astrology. You will become more self-accepting and empowered the more you explore this endless rabbit hole of wisdom. I hope this book has benefited you. Thanks for allowing me to be a part of your astrology journey.

About the Author

Molly McCord, MA, has been studying and professionally practicing Western tropical astrology for over thirty years. She is a bestselling author of eleven books, a professional intuitive astrologer, and a business guide to healers, intuitives, and entrepreneurs. Since 2012, she has offered her weekly astrology podcast with over eight million downloads, aspiring to support astrology enthusiasts and spiritual seekers to deeply connect with their power, choices, and light. Molly holds a bachelor's degree in political science and women's studies and a master's degree in international relations and diplomacy, which have provided unexpected insight into the astrology of our modern times. Visit her at www.mollymccord.online.

San Antonio, TX
www.hierophantpublishing.com